Praise for *Why Read* Moby-Dick*?*

"Exuberant."   —*The Boston Globe*

"[A] slim, passionate manifesto."   —*Chicago Tribune*

"*Why Read* Moby-Dick*?* reels in a compelling case. . . .
Short, lucid, intelligent . . . Philbrick's more like a literary
color analyst, helping readers see the novel better while
also creating a sense of excitement about it."

—*Milwaukee Journal Sentinel*

"This slender, pleasant, sincere book by the maritime his-
torian and naval enthusiast is more than a respectable
tribute unencumbered by academic prose. Approaching
Moby-Dick from outside the academy is refreshing, and
Philbrick's enthusiasm is contagious. . . . So put me down
for a reading of *Moby-Dick* . . . and count Philbrick's book
a success."   —*The New Republic*

PENGUIN BOOKS

WHY READ *MOBY-DICK*?

Nathaniel Philbrick is the author of the acclaimed international bestsellers *In the Heart of the Sea*, which won the National Book Award for nonfiction in 2000; *Sea of Glory: The Epic South Seas Expedition, 1838–42*; *The Last Stand*; *Bunker Hill*; *Away Off Shore*; and *Mayflower*, a finalist for the Pulitzer Prize in History. He is founding director of the Maritime Institute on Nantucket Island and a research fellow at the Nantucket Historical Association. A champion sailboat racer, he has also written extensively about sailing.

WHY READ
MOBY-DICK?

NATHANIEL
PHILBRICK

PENGUIN BOOKS

PENGUIN BOOKS
Published by the Penguin Group
Penguin Group (USA) LLC
375 Hudson Street
New York, New York 10014

USA | Canada | UK | Ireland | Australia | New Zealand | India | South Africa | China
penguin.com
A Penguin Random House Company

First published in the United States of America by Viking Penguin,
a member of Penguin Group (USA) Inc., 2011
Published in Penguin Books 2013

THE LIBRARY OF CONGRESS HAS CATALOGED THE HARDCOVER EDITION AS FOLLOWS
Philbrick, Nathaniel.
Why read Moby-Dick? / Nathaniel Philbrick.
p. cm.
ISBN 978-0-670-02299-1 (hc.)
ISBN 978-0-14-312397-2 (pbk.)
1. Melville, Herman, 1819–1891. Moby Dick. 2. Sea stories, American—
History and criticism. I. Title.
PS2384.M62P55 2011
813'.3—dc22
2011019766

Printed in the United States of America
1   3   5   7   9   10   8   6   4   2

Set in Bulmer MT Std
Designed by Francesca Belanger
Illustrations by Jim Tierney

To Melissa

CONTENTS

Contents

WHY READ
MOBY-DICK?

1

The Gospels in This Century

Early in the afternoon of December 16, 1850, Herman Melville looked at his timepiece. He was in the midst of composing the novel we now know as *Moby-Dick*. At that moment he was writing about how for thousands, even millions of years whales have been filling the atmosphere over the waters of the Pacific with the haze of their spouts—"sprinkling and mystifying the gardens of the deep." It was then that he decided to record the exact time at which he was writing these words about whale spouts: "fifteen and a quarter minutes past one o'clock P.M. of this sixteenth day of December, A.D. 1850."

When *Moby-Dick* was eventually published in November of the following year, the date in this passage was changed from 1850 to 1851. But that is no matter. The fact remains that in this tiny chapter, titled "The Fountain" (the 85th in a novel that would eventually extend to 135 chapters), Melville did something outrageous. He pulled back the fictive curtain and inserted a seemingly irrelevant glimpse of himself in the act of composition.

I've now read *Moby-Dick* at least a dozen times, and this

reference to a specific time and day in December remains my favorite part of the book. Whenever I come upon that sentence, I feel as if I am there, with Melville, as he creates the greatest American novel ever written.

In December 1850, Melville was just thirty-one years old. A few months earlier he'd decided to move his family from New York City to the Berkshires in western Massachusetts, the temporary home of his new literary idol, Nathaniel Hawthorne. Melville was already the father of a baby boy named Malcolm; in October of the following year his wife, Elizabeth, gave birth to a second son, Stanwix.

His literary career had begun in spectacular fashion four years before with *Typee,* a bestseller about his adventures in the South Seas. But Melville quickly learned that success guarantees nothing and in fact turns the future into an endless quest to measure up to the past. As each subsequent book failed to equal *Typee*'s sales, and with his financial responsibilities mounting (his household often included his widowed mother and his sisters), Melville began to worry about the future. "Dollars damn me . . . ," he confided to Hawthorne. "Though I wrote the Gospels in this century, I should die in the gutter."

From the second-floor study of the farmhouse he purchased and renovated with loans from his father-in-law and a family friend, he could see nearby Mount Greylock. When the snow blanketed the surrounding fields that winter, Melville claimed to enjoy "a sort of sea-feeling." But as he worked with an increasing, Ahab-like frenzy on his book about the maimed captain and his pursuit of the White Whale, the omnipresent sea-feeling was anything but a comfort. "My room seems a ship's cabin," he wrote to a literary friend, "& at nights when I wake up & hear the wind shrieking, I almost fancy there is too much sail on the house, & I had better go on the roof & rig in the chimney."

Once seated at his desk each morning, he was literally consumed by his story, sometimes working past four o'clock in the afternoon without pausing to eat. When exhaustion finally forced him to stop, he spent the evening sitting listlessly amid his extended family in what he described as "a sort of mesmeric state." Not only was he drawing upon his own experiences in the Pacific, he was also immersing himself in scientific treatises and narratives associated with the whale fishery. Most important, his recent and omnivorous reading of Shakespeare, Milton, Virgil, and others meant that the voices of these writers were as fresh and accessible to him as anything he might read in a newspaper or magazine.

In 1850 the United States was in the midst of pushing its way west across the full three-thousand-mile breadth of the North American continent. Railroads had begun to knit together the interior of the nation into an iron tracery of ceaseless, smoke-belching movement. Steamboats ventured up once-inaccessible rivers. With the winning of the Mexican War in 1848, America's future as a bicoastal nation was sealed. When word reached the East Coast that gold had been discovered earlier that year in California, thousands upon thousands of prospectors quickly made that future an accomplished fact.

But there was a problem with this juggernaut: a lie festered at the ideological core of the then-thirty states of America. Even though its founders had promised liberty and freedom for all, the southern half of the country was economically dependent on African slavery. Ever since the signing of the Declaration of Independence, the issue had been gnawing at the heart of America, and now, after decades of avoidance and evasion, it was becoming clear that the nation was headed for a crisis. With the passage of the Fugitive Slave Act in 1850, which required that escaped slaves found anywhere in the United States be handed over to the authorities, slavery was no longer just a Southern problem. All Americans, both above and below the Mason-Dixon Line, were now legally bound to the institution of slavery. Antagonisms that had lain dormant for decades could no longer be contained, and an eruption of terrible violence appeared inevitable. Despite all its brilliant successes, America was on the verge of a cataclysm.

To be an American writer in 1850 was to be part of a young, still tentative literary tradition. Washington Irving and James Fenimore Cooper were approaching the ends of their careers, while the poet William Cullen Bryant was one of the most influential literary figures of the time, thanks, in large part, to his position as editor of a leading New York City newspaper. Before his death in 1849, Edgar Allan Poe had pronounced the now-forgotten Southern novelist William

Gilmore Simms "immeasurably the best writer of fiction in America." In the meantime, the poet Henry Wadsworth Longfellow was well on his way to becoming the most popular and best-paid author in America.

But it was British writers such as Charles Dickens and Edward Bulwer-Lytton (known primarily today for beginning one of his novels with the immortal phrase "It was a dark and stormy night") who were the most widely read in the United States. Cooper and Irving had managed to support themselves (sometimes just barely) through their writing, but they were very much the exceptions to the rule. The popular essayist and poet Ralph Waldo Emerson relied on his lecture fees to keep body and soul together, and even Nathaniel Hawthorne, whose *Scarlet Letter* had been selling briskly since its appearance in March of that year, had been employed, until just recently, as a surveyor at the customs house in Salem, Massachusetts. By purchasing a home in the wilds of western Massachusetts with the intention of supporting himself and his family on the income derived from a novel about, of all things, whaling, Melville was embarking on a quest as audacious and doomed as anything dreamed up by the captain of the *Pequod*.

To write timelessly about the here and now, a writer must approach the present indirectly. The story has to be about more than it at first seems. Shakespeare used the historical sources of his plays as a scaffolding on which to construct detailed portraits of his own age. The interstices between the secondhand historical plots and Shakespeare's startlingly original insights into Elizabethan England are what allow his work to speak to us today. Reading Shakespeare, we know what it is like, in any age, to be alive. So it is with *Moby-Dick,* a novel about a whaling voyage to the Pacific that is also about America racing hell-bent toward the Civil War and so much more. Contained in the pages of *Moby-Dick* is nothing less than the genetic code of America: all the promises, problems, conflicts, and ideals that contributed to the outbreak of a revolution in 1775 as well as a civil war in 1861 and continue to drive this country's ever-contentious march into the future. This means that whenever a new crisis grips this country, *Moby-Dick* becomes newly important. It is why subsequent generations have seen Ahab as Hitler during World War II or as a profit-crazed deep-drilling oil company in 2010 or as a power-crazed Middle Eastern dictator in 2011.

The irony is that when *Moby-Dick* was first published in the fall of 1851, virtually no one, except for the author to whom the novel was dedicated, Nathaniel Hawthorne, and his wife, Sophia, seems to have taken much notice. By the time of Melville's death in 1891, *Moby-Dick* had sold a grand total of 3,715 copies. (As a point of comparison, *Typee* sold 16,320 copies.) It wasn't until after World War I that what had begun as a few belated plaudits by some Canadian and English readers had become a virtual tidal wave of praise. There were still some naysayers (Joseph Conrad ridiculed *Moby-Dick* for its romantic, overblown prose), but the vast majority of writers who encountered this improbable book in the first half of the twentieth century were stunned and deeply influenced by how Melville conveyed the specifics of a past world even as he luxuriated in the flagrant and erratic impulses of his own creative process. In its willful refusal to follow the usual conventions of nineteenth-century fiction, *Moby-Dick* possessed the experimental swagger that so many authors were attempting to capture in the years after World War I.

Among the expatriates in Paris in the 1920s, *Moby-Dick* became what one writer described as "a sort of cunning test by which the genuineness of another man's response to literature could be proved." In 1927, William Faulkner, who would later hang a framed print of Rockwell Kent's *Captain Ahab* in his living room in Oxford, Mississippi, claimed that *Moby-Dick* was the one novel by another author that he wished he had written. In 1949, the ever-competitive Ernest Hemingway wrote to his publisher Charles Scribner that as he approached the end of his career, Melville was one of the handful of writers he was still trying to beat.

By 1951, when the centennial of the novel's publication was celebrated throughout the world, Melville's masterpiece had succeeded in becoming more than a literary sensation; it was part of the popular culture. Despite being the author of that most landlocked of American novels, *The Grapes of Wrath*, John Steinbeck had a house in the former whaling port of Sag Harbor on Long Island, and in the 1960s he was the honorary chairman of the Old Whalers Festival, which featured a floating, propeller-driven version of the White Whale known as "Mobile Dick." The novel has inspired plays, films, operas, comic books, a television miniseries, and even a pop-up book. Those who have never read a word of it know the story of Ahab and the White Whale.

Moby-Dick may be well known, but of the handful of novels considered American classics, such as *The Adventures of Huckleberry Finn* and *The Great Gatsby,* it is the most reluctantly read. It is too long and too maddeningly digressive to be properly appreciated by a sleep-deprived adolescent, particularly in this age of digital distractions. I know that as a high school senior in Pittsburgh, Pennsylvania, in 1974, I had expected to be bored to death by the book. But then came that three-word first sentence—"Call me Ishmael"—and I was hooked.

But I had my own reasons for almost instantly falling in love with *Moby-Dick.* On the first page, Ishmael describes the city of New York on a Sunday afternoon, its cooped-up inhabitants lingering on the waterfront, looking out longingly toward the sea in search of the "ungraspable phantom of life." For me, a city kid who had developed an unlikely infatuation with sailing, this scene spoke with a direct, almost overwhelming power. Many of my classmates, however, did not share my enthusiasm, and looking back, I can hardly blame them.

But the novel, like all great works of art, grows on you. Instead of being a page-turner, the book is a repository not only of American history and culture but also of the essentials of Western literature. It has a voice that is one of the most nuanced in all of literature: at once confiding, funny, and oracular—an outpouring of irrepressible eloquence that soars into the stratosphere even as it remains rooted to the ground. The book is so encyclopedic and detailed that space aliens could use it to re-create the whale fishery as it once existed on the planet Earth in the middle of the nineteenth century.

In the more than 150 years since the novel's publication, we have become those space aliens, the inhabitants of a planet so altered by our profligate presence that we are living on a different Earth from the one Melville knew. And yet the more our world changes, the more relevant the novel seems to be. If *Moby-Dick* should, like so many works of literature, fall by the wayside, we will have lost the one book that deserves to be called our American bible. As individuals trying to find our way through the darkness, as citizens of a nation trying to live up to the ideals set forth in our constitution, we need, more than ever before, *Moby-Dick*.

I am not one of those purists who insist on reading the entire untruncated text at all costs. *Moby-Dick* is a long book, and time is short. Even a sentence, a mere phrase, will do. The important thing is to spend some time with the novel, to listen as you read, to feel the prose adapt to the various voices that flowed through Melville during the book's composition like intermittent ghosts with something urgent and essential to say.

What follows is my idiosyncratic answer to the question that serves as this little book's title. As a resident of Nantucket

Island, the holy ground of *Moby-Dick,* and the author of a book about the real-life nautical disaster that inspired the conclusion of the novel, I have my own prejudices and point of view. Perhaps because my parents named me for the author who served as Melville's muse, Nathaniel Hawthorne, I am as intrigued by the events that made possible the book's composition as I am by the book itself. I am also interested in how the novel continued to haunt Melville in the months and years after its publication. Most of all, however, I am interested in getting you—yes, *you*—to read, whether it be for the first time or the twelfth time, *Moby-Dick*.

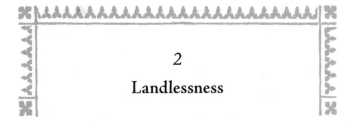

2
Landlessness

In January 1841, Herman Melville shipped out on the *Acush-net* from Fairhaven, Massachusetts, just across the river from the whaling port of New Bedford. His father, a well-liked but ineffectual merchant, had died when Herman was twelve, plunging the family into humiliating poverty. In the eight years since, everything Melville tried, from working as a clerk at a law firm to teaching school to making his fortune in what was then the American wilderness of Illinois and Missouri, had failed. With the economy sunk in depression and with no job prospects, Melville did what the narrator, Ishmael, decides to do at the beginning of *Moby-Dick;* he went to sea.

Almost as soon as the *Acushnet* set sail, Melville began to hear stories about the *Essex,* a Nantucket whaleship that had been sunk more than two decades before by an infuriated sperm whale about a thousand miles west of the Galápagos Islands. Seven months after departing from Fairhaven, the *Acushnet* was approaching the very latitude in the South Pacific on which the *Essex* had gone down when the lookout sighted another whaleship. It turned out to be the *Lima* from

Nantucket. During what was known as a gam, a meeting of two or more whaleships at sea, the crews were given the opportunity to mingle and talk, and Melville was introduced to the son of Owen Chase, first mate of the *Essex* and the author of a narrative about the disaster.

Chase's son offered to lend Melville his copy of his father's book. That night Melville read the story of how an eighty-five-foot bull sperm whale crushed the bow of the *Essex* into splintered fragments and how after taking to three twenty-five-foot whaleboats, the twenty-man crew discussed what to do next. Given the direction of the wind, the obvious next move was to sail to the islands to the west, the closest being the Marquesas. But Chase and his shipmates had heard rumors of cannibals on those islands. Better to sail to a civilized port on the western coast of South America, even if it was against the wind and more than three thousand miles away.

Three months later, when just five survivors were plucked from two sun-scorched, barnacle-encrusted whaleboats, they were no longer the same men who'd refused to sail to an island of hypothetical savages. They had become what they most feared. As made plain by the human bones found in the hands of two of the survivors, they were cannibals. Melville later wrote, "The reading of this wondrous story upon the landless sea, & close to the very latitude of the shipwreck had a surprising effect upon me."

Almost a year later, Melville first glimpsed the islands that the crew of the *Essex* had chosen to spurn. On June 23, 1842, the *Acushnet* arrived at Nuku Hiva, part of the Marquesas group. Melville and the rest of the crew stared at the green spectacular peaks as swimming native women surrounded the ship. According to Melville's later, inevitably fictionalized account of his adventures, the whaleship's deck quickly became crowded with these beautiful young girls, who offered themselves to the sailors for bits of cloth. Not long after, Melville decided he would do exactly the opposite of what Owen Chase and the other crew members of the *Essex* had done. He would desert the ship that had been his home for the last nineteen months and live among the so-called cannibals.

Nine years later he published *Moby-Dick,* a novel that begins with the protagonist, Ishmael, finding himself, to his initial horror, sharing a bed with a tattooed cannibal named Queequeg. In a winningly comic distillation of the experience that had forever changed Melville's life in the Marquesas, Ishmael comes to the realization that artificial distinctions between civilization and savagery are beside the point. "What's all this fuss I have been making about, thought I to myself— the man's a human being just as I am: he has just as much reason to fear me, as I have to be afraid of him. Better sleep with a sober cannibal than a drunken Christian." This startling insight was revolutionary in 1851 and is still wickedly fresh to us today, more than 150 years later, as globalization makes encounters with foreign cultures an almost daily occurrence.

But Melville was not able to laugh away the lessons of the *Essex.* Despite its comic beginning, *Moby-Dick* quickly moves into darker and more harrowing metaphysical territory, and it is the moral isolation of the *Essex* crew members, afloat upon the wide and immense sea in their tiny whaleboats, that underlies the fated voyage of the *Pequod*. In the chapter "The Lee Shore," Ishmael speaks of one Bulkington, a sailor for whom the land has proved "scorching to his feet" and who heads out once again after just completing a previous whaling voyage. It is only amid the terrifying vastness of the sea that man can confront the ultimate truths of his existence: "[A]ll deep, earnest thinking is but the intrepid effort of the soul to keep the open independence of her sea. . . . [I]n landlessness alone resides the highest truth, shoreless, indefinite as God. . . . Terrors of the terrible! is all this agony so vain?" For Melville, and for any thinking human being, this is more than a rhetorical question.

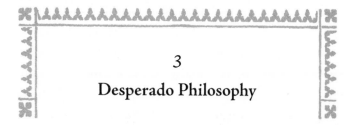

3

Desperado Philosophy

He tells us to call him Ishmael, but who is the narrator of *Moby-Dick*? For one thing, he has known depression, "a damp, drizzly November in my soul." But he is also a person of genuine enthusiasms. Like Holden Caulfield in *The Catcher in the Rye,* he is wonderfully engaging, a vulnerable wiseass who invites us to join him on a quest to murder the blues by shipping out on a whaleship.

Ishmael is no tourist. As a common seaman, he gets paid for his adventures. "[B]*eing paid,*" he rhapsodizes, "what will compare with it? The urbane activity with which a man receives money is really marvellous, considering that we so earnestly believe money to be the root of all earthly ills, and that on no account can a monied man enter heaven. Ah! how cheerfully we consign ourselves to perdition!"

Getting paid is certainly a bonus, but Ishmael isn't doing this for the money. He's in pursuit of an almost Platonic ideal, what he calls "the overwhelming idea of the great whale himself." "Such a portentous and mysterious monster," he continues, "roused all my curiosity." But he's also looking for the clarifying jolt that comes with doing something dangerous. "I love to sail forbidden seas," he tells us, "and land on barbarous coasts." The best way to satisfy this "everlasting itch for things remote," he decides, is to head for Nantucket, the birthplace of American whaling. "[T]here was a fine, boisterous something about everything connected with that famous old island," he says, "which amazingly pleased me."

Not even a sobering visit to the Seamen's Bethel in New Bedford, where he studies the marble tablets memorializing those lost at sea, is enough to make him rethink his decision to ship out on a Nantucket vessel. "Yes, there is death in this business of whaling—a speechlessly quick chaotic bundling of a man into Eternity. But what then?"

A reckless, rapturous sense of his soul's imperishability overtakes Ishmael. "Methinks my body is but the lees [the sediment left in wine] of my better being. In fact take my body who will, take it I say, it is not me." Let God, fate, or what have you do as it sees fit. In the end, Ishmael will prevail. "And therefore three cheers for Nantucket," he exults, "and come a stove boat and stove body when they will, for stave my soul, Jove himself cannot."

Later in the book, after he is almost killed when his whale-boat is smacked by a whale before being swamped in a squall, Ishmael decides it might be a good idea, after all, to write his will. And it is here, in chapter 49, "The Hyena," that he hits upon the approach to life that will act as the emotional and philosophical center of the novel. "There are certain queer times and occasions in this strange mixed affair we call life," he tells us, "when a man takes this whole universe for a vast practical joke, though the wit thereof he but dimly discerns, and more than suspects that the joke is at nobody's expense but his own."

Ishmael describes this approach to life as a "free and easy sort of genial, desperado philosophy." In the chapters to come, Ahab will drag him (and all of us) into the howling depths of the human psyche. In the beginning, however, before Ahab takes hold, we are in the presence of a soul so buoyant, so mischievous, so wise, and so much fun that even after the worst happens at the end of the novel, we can take consolation in knowing that at least Ishmael has found a way to survive. Like Melville, who is one of our country's greatest literary survivors, Ishmael is still left to tell the tale, and we had better listen to every word.

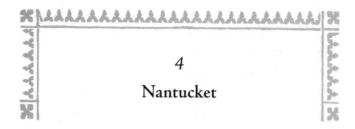

4

Nantucket

When Melville wrote *Moby-Dick,* New Bedford, not Nantucket, was the most important whaling port in America. But Ishmael is not interested in the biggest whaling port; he wants to go to the first, to the "great original," the sandy island almost thirty miles out to sea where it all began.

Melville drew upon his own personal experiences in his novels, but he was also a great pillager of other writers' prose. During the composition of *Moby-Dick* he acquired a virtual library of whaling-related books, and passages from these works inevitably made their way into his novel. The writing process for Melville was as much about responding to and incorporating the works of others as it was about relying on his own experiences. And since Melville seems never to have visited Nantucket before writing *Moby-Dick,* he was free to create an imagined rather than an actual island, an animated, often antic state of mind that exemplified America's grasping push for more. And since Nantucket in 1850 was already past its prime, there is a nostalgic quality to his five-paragraph evocation of the island in chapter 14. Instead of writing history, Melville is forging an American mythology.

Nantucket, Ishmael proclaims, is "a mere hillock, and elbow of sand; all beach, without a background." He then proceeds to spin off joke after joke about how sandy and sterile the island is. There are so few trees on Nantucket that islanders carry around scraps of wood "like bits of the true cross in Rome." They plant toadstools to provide themselves with some shade. In order to wade through all the sand, they wear the gritty equivalent of snowshoes. The sea is so omnipresent "that to their very chairs and tables small clams will sometimes be found adhering."

After devoting the two subsequent paragraphs to a distillation of the island's history, taking us from the oral traditions of the first Native inhabitants through to the islanders' current pursuit of "[t]hat Himmalehan, salt-sea Mastodon," he establishes Nantucket as a nodal point of global, God-ordained ambition. "And thus have these naked Nantucketers, these sea hermits, issuing from their ant-hill in the sea, overrun and conquered the watery world like so many Alexanders; parcelling out among them the Atlantic, Pacific, and Indian oceans, as the three pirate powers did Poland. Let America add Mexico to Texas, and pile Cuba upon Canada; let the English overswarm all India, and hang out their blazing banner from the sun; two thirds of this terraqueous globe are the Nantucketer's. For the sea is his; he owns it, as Emperors own empires."

The Nantucketer does not just sail across the ocean; he lives upon it in his quest for the sperm whale. "*There* is his home; *there* lies his business, which a Noah's flood would not interrupt, though it overwhelmed all the millions in China." These are not people of the real world; these are the argonauts of their day, superheroes impervious to the worst that God has heaped upon humanity. Then there is the chapter's beautiful, carefully modulated final sentence: "With the landless gull, that at sunset folds her wings and is rocked to sleep between billows; so at nightfall, the Nantucketer, out of sight of land, furls his sails, and lays him to his rest, while under his very pillow rush herds of walruses and whales." And so it ends, this little sidebar of miraculous prose, one of many that Melville scatters like speed bumps throughout the book as he purposely slows the pace of his mighty novel to a magisterial crawl.

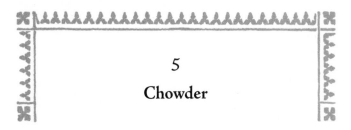

5

Chowder

The Nantucket of chapter 14 is a euphoric whirlwind. The "real" Nantucket, at least the town in which Ishmael and Queequeg soon find themselves, is anything but boisterous and fun. It is a shadow land made of Melville's worst nightmares, the breeding ground of the ominous cloud out of which Ahab will eventually stump forth on his whalebone leg.

Before we get into all that, however, we must linger over one of the more tangible gifts Melville provides in *Moby-Dick:* his recipe for clam chowder. Ishmael and Queequeg have just found their way to the Try Pots Inn, named for the huge iron cauldrons in which the whale's blubber was boiled into oil. There they enjoy bowl after bowl of Mrs. Hussey's chowder. "Oh, sweet friends!" Ishmael crows with delight. "[H]earken to me. It was made of small juicy clams, scarcely bigger than hazel nuts, mixed with pounded ship biscuit, and salted pork cut up into little flakes; the whole enriched with butter, and plentifully seasoned with pepper and salt." Remember this, all ye modern-day chowder makers, forgo the cloying chunks of needless potato and go with the biscuit bits!

Even before they enter the Try Pots, Ishmael has begun to wonder what he's gotten himself into. The inn's sign, made from a sawed-off topmast, reminds him of a gallows. Then there's the name of the man who recommended this establishment, I. A. Coffin. He cannot help but suspect that these are "oblique hints touching Tophet." While leading them to their room, Mrs. Hussey tells the story of "young Stiggs," the whaleman who, after returning from a four-year voyage with only three barrels of oil, stabbed himself to death with his own harpoon. "[E]ver since then," Mrs. Hussey explains, "I allow no boarders to take sich dangerous weepons in their rooms a-night."

The next day, Ishmael leaves Queequeg in their room praying to his tiny wooden idol, Yojo. When he returns that evening, he finds the door locked. Queequeg does not answer his increasingly anxious knocks, and Ishmael, aided and abetted by Mrs. Hussey, begins to fear the worst. Queequeg has killed himself. "It's unfort'nate Stiggs done over again . . . ," Mrs. Hussey wails. "God pity his poor mother!" In desperation, Ishmael shoulders open the door, only to find Queequeg still squatting trancelike before his wooden idol.

A similar drama was enacted every day in the Melville household during the composition of *Moby-Dick*. Locked in his room, Melville routinely ignored attempts by his family members to offer him some lunch. In the years to come, his very Mrs. Hussey–like mother feared that her son's commitment to writing was not good for his sanity, a concern Ishmael echoes soon after discovering Queequeg: "I began to grow vexed with him; it seemed so downright senseless and insane to be sitting there all day and half the night on his hams in a cold room, holding a piece of wood on his head." These are sentiments to which the parent (or spouse) of any writer can relate.

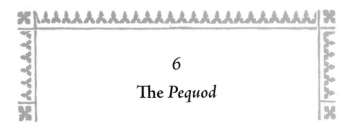

6

The *Pequod*

Time passes, fashions come and go, and the past becomes its own hermetically sealed world. It's easy to laugh at those people under figurative glass, or, even worse, to revere them as exempt from the complexities of our own age. Baloney. Life is life, and the world Melville describes in *Moby-Dick* is as cutting-edge, confused, and *out-there* as anything we can dream up in our own time. Take, for example, the square-rigged, bluff-bowed whaleship.

Simple and cheap to build, it lasted for decades and could sail around the world without using a jot of carbon-based fuel. It was home to a crew of between twenty and thirty-five sailors who regularly pursued the largest game the world has ever known. If the whalemen were lucky enough to kill one of these creatures, the deck of the ship became a slippery slaughterhouse as the gigantic corpse was hacked into pieces for processing. With the firing up of the chimneylike tryworks, the ship was transformed into a refinery, and the greasy, foul-smelling whale blubber became oil. The sale of this yellowish fluid, stored in wooden casks and used to light the streets of major cities and lubricate the machines of the emerging Industrial Age, made the predominantly Quaker whaling merchants of Nantucket some of the richest men in America and the world.

The *Pequod,* the ship that Ishmael chooses for himself and Queequeg, is one of these remarkable, incredibly complex machines, but she is also something more. Just as Nantucket is largely a rhetorical construct, so is the *Pequod* not of this world. She is the mythic incarnation of America: a country blessed by God and by free enterprise that nonetheless embraces the barbarity it supposedly supplanted. The *Pequod* (named for the once-defeated Indian tribe that now owns a highly profitable casino in Connecticut—how Melville would have loved that turn of events!) is an old ship, and she wears her history visibly: "Her ancient decks were worn and wrinkled, like the pilgrim-worshipped flag-stone in Canterbury Cathedral where Becket bled. But to all these her old antiquities, were added new and marvellous features, pertaining to the wild business that for more than half a century she had followed. . . . She was a thing of trophies. A cannibal of a craft, tricking herself forth in the chased bones of her enemies. All round, her unpanelled, open bulwarks were garnished like one continuous jaw, with the long sharp teeth of the sperm whale, inserted there for pins, to fasten her old hempen thews and tendons to. . . . A noble craft, but somehow a most melancholy! All noble things are touched with that."

On the *Pequod*'s weather- and oil-stained deck, her two owners, the Quaker merchants Peleg and Bildad, sheltered in a wigwam made of whalebone, sign on crew members for as little money as possible. Like the United States, a nation devoted to freedom for all that also sanctioned slavery, these two Quaker whalemen—in particular, the pious Bildad—have found a way to accommodate two seemingly irreconcilable principles. "[T]hough a sworn foe to human bloodshed, yet had he . . . spilled tuns upon tuns of leviathan gore." A "Quaker with a vengeance," he also has no qualms about exploiting the whalemen under his employ. Bildad, Ishmael opines, "had long since come to the sage and sensible conclusion that a man's religion is one thing, and this practical world quite another. This world pays dividends."

The compartmentalization of spiritual and worldly concerns is a temptation in every era. In Melville's day, it was most apparent with the issue of slavery, and Bildad, the Bible-reading Quaker whaleman, illustrates the truth of Frederick Douglass's observation that the most brutal slaveholders were always the most devout. "For a pious man," Ishmael says, "especially for a Quaker, [Bildad] was certainly rather hardhearted, to say the least. He never used to swear, though, at his men, they said; but somehow he got an inordinate quantity of cruel, unmitigated hard work out of them."

Melville's years on a whaleship gave him a firsthand appreciation for the backbreaking reality of physical labor. Politicians might speak patriotically about the principles of liberty and freedom, but it was repetitious, soul-crushing work— a form of bodily punishment to which most white Americans refused to submit—that was responsible for the country's prosperity. Once a whale was killed, it took an entire day to process it, a task only to be repeated when another whale was sighted. "Oh! my friends, but this is man-killing!" Ishmael laments. "Yet this is life. For hardly have we mortals by long toilings extracted from this world's vast bulk its small but valuable sperm; and then, with weary patience, cleansed ourselves from its defilements, and learned to live here in clean tabernacles of the soul; hardly is this done, when—*There she blows!*—the ghost is spouted up, and away we sail to fight some other world, and go through young life's old routine again."

The crew of a typical whaleship was made up of men from all over the world. In addition to white sailors from America and Europe, there were Native Americans, African Americans, Azoreans, Cape Verdeans, and South Sea Islanders. The harpooneers aboard the *Pequod* include Queequeg, from the Polynesian island of Kokovoko ("It is not down in any map," Ishmael tells us; "true places never are"); Daggoo, the "imperial negro" from Africa; Tashtego, a Wampanoag from Martha's Vineyard; and Fedallah, the mysterious fire worshipper dressed in a Chinese-style jacket. What distinguishes the thirty crew members of the *Pequod,* Ishmael notes, is that almost all of them, including the officers, many of whom hail from Nantucket, are islanders, what he calls "*Isolatoes* . . . each *Isolato* living on a separate continent of his own. Yet now, federated along one keel . . ."

This demographic diversity was not typical of the United

States in the mid-nineteenth century, when to be an American was to be white and, if not already rich, on the way to wealth as the nation proudly took its place as a global power. A century and a half later, we have a very different perspective on the role of other peoples and cultures in America's rise. As Ishmael notes, the white American "liberally provides the brains, the rest of the world as generously supplying the muscles." Because of his exposure to these various peoples aboard a whaleship, Melville was one of the few authors of his time to have firsthand experience with where the future lay for America in a demographic sense, and his portrayal of working people is never stereotypical or condescending.

Melville was well aware of the great gift he had been given when he shipped out on a whaler. His contemporaries didn't recognize it, but he knew that his experiences in the Pacific had better served his artistic purposes than any education he might have received at a traditional university. Whatever future reputation he might enjoy would depend on his exposure to whaling: "[I]f hereafter I shall do anything that, upon the whole, a man might rather have done than to have left undone," Ishmael tells us, "if, at my death, my executors, or more properly my creditors, find any precious MSS. in my desk, then here I prospectively ascribe all the honor and the glory to whaling; for a whale-ship was my Yale College and my Harvard."

Melville's time aboard a whaler also left him with an appreciation for the liberating power of democracy, what Ishmael calls the "democratic dignity" that distinguished America (with, of course, the notable exception of Southern slavery) from just about every other country in the mid-nineteenth century. In the dangerous work environment of the whale fishery it didn't matter what your race or background was; what mattered was whether you could do your job. At one point the *Pequod*'s third mate, Flask, climbs onto the shoulders of his towering black harpooneer Daggoo so he can get a better view of a pod of whales. "[T]he sight of little Flask mounted upon gigantic Daggoo was yet more curious," Ishmael observes, "for sustaining himself with a cool, indifferent, easy, unthought of, barbaric majesty, the noble negro to every roll of the sea harmoniously rolled his fine form. On his broad back, flaxen-haired Flask seemed a snow-flake. The bearer looked nobler than the rider." In this single image, Melville has managed to illustrate what he calls elsewhere the "divine equality" of humanity even as he provides a scathing critique of slavery. Flask may outrank Daggoo, but it is the African harpooneer who literally carries the third mate on his shoulders.

Democracy in principle, Ishmael maintains, "radiates without end from God; Himself! The great God absolute!" This is not to say, however, that democracy is problem-free. "[T]ake high abstracted man alone," Ishmael says, "and he seems a wonder, a grandeur, and a woe. But from the same point, take mankind in mass, and for the most part, they seem a mob of unnecessary duplicates." For in every age, there will be a threat to the principle of "divine equality," and his name is Ahab.

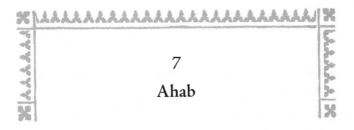

7
Ahab

He doesn't appear until almost a quarter of the way into the book, in chapter 28. Like that of the shark in the movie *Jaws,* his entrance is all the more powerful because of the delay.

Ishmael has just reported on deck for the forenoon watch when he glances aft and sees the *Pequod*'s commander for the first time. Like America in 1850, Ahab is a man divided, seared and parboiled by the conflagration raging inside him. "He looked," Ishmael tells us, "like a man cut away from the stake, when the fire has overrunningly wasted all the limbs without consuming them. . . . Threading its way out from among his grey hairs, and continuing right down one side of his tawny scorched face and neck, till it disappeared in his clothing, you saw a slender rod-like mark, lividly whitish. It resembled that perpendicular seam sometimes made in the straight, lofty trunk of a great tree, when the upper lightning tearingly darts down it, and without wrenching a single twig, peels and grooves out the bark from top to bottom, ere running off into the soil, leaving the tree still greenly alive, but branded."

With his whalebone leg planted in an auger hole in the quarterdeck and grasping a shroud in one of his hands, Ahab scans the ocean ahead. "There was an infinity of firmest fortitude, a determinate, unsurrenderable wilfulness, in the fixed and fearless, forward dedication of that glance." There is also a sad grandeur about the man. Ishmael calls him "moody stricken Ahab . . . with a crucifixion in his face; in all the nameless regal overbearing dignity of some mighty woe."

Gradually, we learn Ahab's backstory. In the days and weeks after losing his leg to the White Whale during his previous voyage, he found his agonies, both physical and mental, unbearable, and his mates had no choice but to "lace him fast, . . . raving in his hammock." As the ship pounded through a succession of terrible gales and Ahab swung back and forth, writhing and screaming within his makeshift straitjacket, a terrible transformation took place within him: "[H]is torn body and gashed soul bled into one another; and so interfusing, made him mad."

In his madness, Ahab came to see Moby Dick as more than a mere whale; he was "the monomaniac incarnation of all those malicious agencies which some deep men feel eating in them, till they are left living on with half a heart and half a lung. . . . [A]ll evil, to crazy Ahab, [was] visibly personified, and made practically assailable in Moby Dick." Once back on

Nantucket, Ahab seemed to have fully recovered his senses. In truth, "his hidden self, raved on," and he resolved to set out on another voyage and kill the White Whale.

To assist him in his deranged quest, Ahab decided to enlist his own whaleboat crew made up of four oarsmen from Manila ("a race," Ishmael claims, "notorious for a certain diabolism of subtilty, and . . . supposed to be the paid spies and secret confidential agents . . . of the devil") and the harpooneer Fedallah, "tall and swart, with one white tooth evilly protruding from [his] steel-like lips." Hidden in the *Pequod*'s hold, Fedallah and his four oarsmen are not revealed to the rest of the ship's crew until the first whale is sighted long after they've left Nantucket.

I must admit that it wasn't until my most recent reading of *Moby-Dick* that I came to appreciate the importance of Fedallah. He and his men from Manila are much more than infernal window dressing. They are essential to what makes Ahab Ahab because no leader, no matter how deranged, is without his inner circle of advisers, the handlers who keep him on task.

We never find out the details of how Ahab first met Fedallah, but we do learn that something unspeakably strange happened to the *Pequod*'s captain prior to the ship's departure from Nantucket. Ishmael reports that he was found lying on the ground, with his whalebone leg "violently displaced" and driven "stake-wise" into his groin. The victim of an apparent accident, Ahab in his agonizing helplessness has yet another debilitating injury to blame on Moby Dick. Whether or not this humiliating mishap convinced him that he needed supernatural support, one thing does become clear: no crew member aboard the *Pequod* is more important to Ahab than the turbaned soothsayer Fedallah.

8

The Anatomy of a Demagogue

To be in the presence of a great leader is to know a blighted soul who has managed to make the darkness work for him. Ishmael says it best: "For all men tragically great are made so through a certain morbidness. Be sure of this, O young ambition, all mortal greatness is but disease." In chapter 36, "The Quarter-Deck," Melville shows us how susceptible we ordinary people are to the seductive power of a great and demented man.

At the beginning of the chapter, Ahab seethes with barely contained energy as he paces back and forth across the deck, the point of his whalebone leg leaving the wood "dented, like geological stones." Stubb, the second mate, observes that "the chick that's in him pecks the shell." And then it begins, Ahab's version of a command performance. Until this point, he has not revealed the secret purpose of the voyage. What he wants to do is illegal. He has not been hired by the *Pequod*'s owners to revenge himself on a white whale. However, if he can win the crew and his pliable second and third mates to his pur-

⸺, perhaps he can bulldoze the first mate, Starbuck, into accepting the inevitable.

He orders Starbuck to "send everybody aft." Once the crew has been gathered before him, he continues to pace back and forth. Only after their curiosity has been suitably aroused does he begin by asking an unexpected question. "What do ye do when ye see a whale, men?" "Sing out for him!" is the immediate reply.

For a demagogue, it's the oldest trick in the book. With each question and response, the crowd cannot help but be wooed to the speaker's enthusiastic purpose. "[M]ariners began to gaze curiously at each other," Ishmael relates, "as if marvelling how it was that they themselves became so excited at such seemingly purposeless questions." This is the dynamic of the political rally, the kind of rhetorically fueled gathering that Melville's older brother Gansevoort, a low-level Democratic Party operative, helped organize during his abbreviated political career. It is also the dynamic of the revival meetings of the Second Great Awakening, which swept across America during the first half of the nineteenth century and which contributed, in turn, to the growing evangelical fervor of the abolitionist movement in the years prior to the Civil War.

Now that Ahab has the ship's crew in his power, he brings out a prop: a gold doubloon. He then orders Starbuck to give him a hammer, and as he prepares to nail the coin to the mast, he tells them that the first person to see "a white-headed whale with a wrinkled brow and a crooked jaw" will get the coin. The crowd goes wild. "'Huzza! huzza!' cried the seamen, as with swinging tarpaulins they hailed the act of nailing the gold to the mast."

The harpooneers, it turns out, have all, at one time or another, seen this notorious whale. "Death and devils!" Ahab exults. "[M]en, it is Moby Dick ye have seen—Moby Dick— Moby Dick!"

At that moment, Starbuck puts two and two together. "Captain Ahab, I have heard of Moby Dick—but it was not Moby Dick that took off thy leg?"

Ahab had apparently hoped to leave out this particular detail. "Who told thee that?" he spits out. But after a brief pause he decides that instead of denying the truth, he'll make the truth work for him. "Aye, Starbuck," he acknowledges, "aye, my hearties all round; it was Moby Dick that dismasted me; Moby Dick that brought me to this dead stump I stand on now." And then he does what only the best politician can do; he sheds a tear. "'Aye, aye,' he shouted with a terrific, loud, animal sob, like that of a heart-stricken moose . . . ; 'Aye, aye! and I'll chase him round Good Hope, and round the Horn, and round the Norway Maelstrom, and round perdition's flames before I give him up. And this is what ye have shipped for, men! to chase that white whale on both sides of land, and over all sides of earth, till he spouts black blood and rolls fin out. What say ye, men, will ye splice hands on it, now? I think ye do look brave.'"

This is the pivotal moment. But Ahab needn't have worried. "'Aye, aye!' shouted the harpooneers and seamen, running closer to the excited old man: 'A sharp eye for the White Whale; a sharp lance for Moby Dick!'"

"God bless ye," Ahab says with a "half sob and half shout," before ordering the steward to serve the men some grog. He then turns to the first mate. "But what's this long face about, Mr. Starbuck; wilt thou not chase the white whale? art not game for Moby Dick?"

Starbuck responds by asking what Ahab's vengeance will get "in our Nantucket market." It's then, to borrow from the movie *This Is Spinal Tap,* that Ahab dials his charisma to eleven. "But come closer, Starbuck," he says, "thou requirest a little lower layer." It's not about the money, he explains; this is personal. Thumping his chest, he cries out, "[M]y vengeance will fetch a great premium *here!*"

Starbuck is quite rightly appalled. "To be enraged with a dumb thing, Captain Ahab," he sputters, "seems blasphemous." This prompts Ahab to reveal the logic, such as it is, behind his campaign against the White Whale. According to Ahab, Moby Dick is not just a sperm whale; he is the tool of an unseen and decidedly evil power. "All visible objects . . . ," Ahab insists, "are but as pasteboard masks." By killing Moby Dick, he will punch through the mask and get at the root cause of all his unhappiness and pain. He then compares the world to a jail cell. "How can the prisoner reach outside except by thrusting through the wall? To me, the white whale is that wall, shoved near to me." Unlocking the secrets of the universe by killing a whale doesn't make much sense, but what good is rationality to a man possessed by such a terrifying and all-devouring rage? "He tasks me; he heaps me," Ahab cries. "I see in him outrageous strength, with an inscrutable malice sinewing it. That inscrutable thing is chiefly what I hate; and be the white whale agent, or be the white whale principal, I will wreak that hate upon him. Talk not to me of blasphemy, man; I'd strike the sun if it insulted me."

He then directs Starbuck's attention to the rest of the crew, all of whom are "one and all with Ahab." And besides, he continues, what's so terrible about pursuing a white whale; isn't whale killing what it's all about? "'Tis but to help strike a fin," he insists, "no wondrous feat for Starbuck."

Ahab finally appeals to Starbuck's not inconsiderable vanity as a whaleman. "From this one poor hunt, then, the best lance out of all Nantucket, surely he will not hang back?" When the first mate does not immediately respond, Ahab knows he has him. "Starbuck now is mine," he exults. What Ahab does not hear as he savors "his joy at the enchanted, tacit acquiescence" is Starbuck's murmured "God keep me!—keep us all!" as well as the flap of the sails as the wind suddenly vanishes and, most disturbing of all, "the low laugh from the hold" of Fedallah.

Once the grog has been passed around and the harpooneers have sworn their allegiance with a toast drunk from their harpoon sockets, Ahab retires to his cabin, where he watches the sun set outside the stern windows and reflects on what transpired on the quarterdeck. "'Twas not so hard a task," he soliloquizes. "I thought to find one stubborn, at the least; but my one cogged circle fits into all their various wheels, and they revolve. . . . What I've dared, I've willed; and what I've willed, I'll do! They think me mad—Starbuck does; but I'm demoniac, I am madness maddened!"

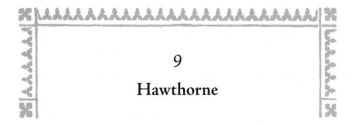

9

Hawthorne

So where did it come from, this darkness, this witchy voodoo of the void? As it turns out, Melville's incomparable ability to humanize evil came from a most unlikely, late-breaking source: a shy, soft-spoken writer named Nathaniel Hawthorne, whom Melville didn't meet until he was almost done with the first draft. The story of their friendship and especially the letters from Melville that it produced are reason enough to read *Moby-Dick,* a novel that is as much about the microclimates of intimate human relations as it is about the great, uncontrollable gales that push and pull all of us.

In the late summer of 1850, Melville thought he was finished with his whaling novel, a book that apparently hadn't a whiff of Ahab in it. In early August, Melville's guest in Pittsfield, Massachusetts, Evert Duyckinck, reported to his wife that his host was "mostly done" with "a romantic, fanciful & literal & most enjoyable presentment of the Whale Fishery." Then, on August 5, Melville met Nathaniel Hawthorne.

At forty-six, Hawthorne was fifteen years Melville's senior. He'd recently completed *The Scarlet Letter* and was now working on *The House of the Seven Gables* in a rented farm-house in nearby Lenox, where he lived with his wife, Sophia, and their two children, Julian and Una. During a picnic atop Monument Mountain, the two writers had a chance to talk for the first time. Soon after, Melville read Hawthorne's story collection *Mosses from an Old Manse*. A week later, Melville gave Duyckinck the essay "Hawthorne and His Mosses" for publication in the *Literary World*.

At that time, Hawthorne enjoyed a reputation as a mild-mannered recluse penning well-crafted stories about New England's quaint colonial past. This, Melville insisted, was missing the point. Instead of a "harmless" stylist, Hawthorne was an unappreciated genius possessed by "this great power of blackness." Hidden beneath his stories' lapidarian surfaces were truths so profound and disturbing that they ranked with anything written in the English language.

Melville then turned his attention in the review to Shakespeare. "[I]t is those deep far-away things in him," Melville declared, "those occasional flashings-forth of the intuitive Truth in him; those short, quick probings at the very axis of reality;—these are the things that make Shakespeare, Shakespeare." Moreover, it was through his "dark characters," such as Hamlet, Lear, and Iago, that Shakespeare "craftily says, or sometimes insinuates the things, which we feel to be so terrifically true, that it were all but madness for any good man, in his own proper character, to utter, or even hint of them!" In writing about Hawthorne, Melville, via Shakespeare, was laying the groundwork for Ahab.

During the fall of 1850, Melville and Hawthorne got to know each other. Temperamentally, the two men could not have been more different. Melville, Sophia Hawthorne wrote, was a "man . . . with life to his finger-tips." Hawthorne, on the other hand, preferred to keep life at a distance. In fact, Sophia confessed in a letter to her mother that prior to meeting Melville on Monument Mountain, her "shy dear" of a husband had specifically requested *not* to be introduced to the young and enthusiastic writer. Even in friendship, Hawthorne remained remote and detached while Melville was always crowding in. "Nothing pleases me better," Sophia wrote of their new literary friend, "than to sit & hear this growing man dash his tumultuous waves of thought up against Mr. Hawthorne's great, genial, comprehending silences."

But Melville was not all ardent impetuosity in his conversations with Hawthorne; there was, as Sophia observed, a somewhat unsettling method to his madness. In a letter to her mother, Sophia revealed that the one thing she didn't like about Melville was his "small eyes." "Once in a while," she explained, "his animation gives place to a singularly quiet expression, out of those eyes to which I have objected; an indrawn, dim look, but which at the same time makes you feel that he is at that instant taking deepest note of what is before him. It is a strange, lazy glance, but with a power in it quite unique. It does not seem to penetrate through you, but to take you into itself." This is Melville caught in the act of creative infiltration—the sneaky, deceptively "lazy" way that he took what he needed from Hawthorne. Instead of a literary influence, Hawthorne was, for Melville, more of a source of emotional inspiration: the figure that moved him to take Shakespeare's lead and dive into the darkness. Just as Ahab co-opted the *Pequod*, Melville used Hawthorne's fiction only as it served his own literary purposes.

But what about Hawthorne the man? Where did the power of darkness come from? Melville was at a loss. "Whether Hawthorne has simply availed himself of this mystical blackness as a means to the wondrous effects he makes . . . ," Melville wrote in his review, "or whether there really lurks in him, perhaps unknown to himself, a touch of Puritanic gloom,—this, I cannot altogether tell." "[T]here is something lacking—a good deal lacking," Melville wrote in February 1851 to Duyckinck, "to the plump sphericity of the man. What is that?—He doesn't patronise the butcher—he needs roast-beef, done rare." What Hawthorne needed, more than anything else, was a cannibal friend like Queequeg.

Late in life, long after Hawthorne's death at fifty-nine, Melville told his son, Julian, that he believed his father "had all his life concealed some great secret, which would, were it known, explain all the mysteries of his career." The essential inscrutability of Hawthorne is everywhere in *Moby-Dick*—in Ahab's agonizing need to know what is really behind the world's "pasteboard masks," in the way the White Whale resonates with fearful and fantastic possibilities and yet ultimately reveals nothing.

Prior to meeting Hawthorne, Melville had been churning out novels at such a furious rate (he'd penned his most recent two books in a matter of months) that his British publisher advised him to slow down. Under the steadying influence of Hawthorne, Melville paused in the middle of a quite ordinary, picaresque novel about whaling and completely rethought the story in terms of the power of darkness he recognized in Hawthorne's short stories. Only then did he plunge once again into his whaling material, this time creating the masterpiece for which he will always be remembered.

Through Ahab, Melville found a way to articulate what he called in his review of Hawthorne "the sane madness of vital truth," those Tourette's-like outbursts that no one wants to hear, especially since they happen to be true. If a life amounts only to a senseless death, what is a person to do? Ahab has decided that the best and noblest option available under the circumstances is to attack some substitute for this absurd and ultimately amoral life, such as a white whale, and hurl all his rage and fear and hate at this *thing* even if he knows, in his heart of hearts, that it will lead not only to his own death but to the deaths of those who follow him.

One of the reasons Ahab is such a compelling character is that Melville saw much of himself in the captain's tendency to regard the world symbolically. This is the tendency Melville had to battle throughout his literary career as his metaphysical preoccupations perpetually threatened to overwhelm his unsurpassed ability to find the specific, concrete detail that conveys everything. He also identified with Ahab's outrageous ambition, for Melville was, he at least hoped, creating a "mighty book."

The other breakthrough associated with his invention of Ahab was something he clearly got from Hawthorne: a way to put artistic distance between himself and the very thing he most identified with, thus providing a way to write about the darkest and most frightening aspects of human experience. That was why he could write to Hawthorne, "I have written a wicked book, and feel spotless as the lamb."

Ultimately, however, Melville had difficulty maintaining Hawthorne's cool remove from the darkness. As Sophia Hawthorne observed, Melville engaged with life; he also engaged with his characters. In December 1850, as he rebuilt his novel on the blasted, ripped-apart foundations of the first draft, he wrote to Duyckinck about the difficulties of transferring what he had in his head onto the page: "And taking a book off the brain, is akin to the ticklish & dangerous business of taking an old painting off a panel—you have to scrape off the whole brain in order to get at it with due safety—& even then, the painting may not be worth the trouble." As suggested by this letter, the process of creating Ahab, of channeling what Melville later called "my evil art," was an all-involving and psychically corrosive experience. If bits of his brain matter were not literally being left upon the manuscript pages of *Moby-Dick*, something nonetheless was happening to him during those winter and spring months in his study.

The eyes that so troubled Sophia Hawthorne began to bother Melville to the point that he could barely see the words he was writing on the page. In *Pierre*, the novel he wrote after *Moby-Dick*, he provides a fictionalized account of the torment he suffered in his second-story room: "His incessant application told upon his eyes. They became so affected, that some days he wrote with the lids nearly closed, fearful of opening them wide to the light. . . . Sometimes he blindly wrote with his eyes turned away from the paper." His eyes so scalded that he could not even see what he was writing, Melville pushed on toward Ahab's encounter with the White Whale.

10

The View from the Masthead

Ishmael of the Bible was Abraham's bastard son, who along with his servant mother, Hagar, was banished from his father's household and forced to wander the desert. Ishmael of *Moby-Dick* has suffered some grievous unnamed loss and now wanders the waters of the world.

He is not alone in this. As he mentions in chapter 35, "The Mast-Head," a whaleship in the mid-nineteenth century served as "an asylum for many romantic, melancholy, and absent-minded young men, disgusted with the carking cares of earth, and seeking sentiment in tar and blubber." As opposed to Ahab's urgent, soul-singed probing into the meaning of life, Ishmael and his compatriots are more interested in losing themselves in the cosmos. As naive seekers of philosophical truth, their favorite perch is at the masthead on a quiet sunny day in the Pacific.

"There you stand," Ishmael says, "a hundred feet above the silent decks, striding along the deep, as if the masts were gigantic stilts, while beneath you and between your legs, as it were, swim the hugest monsters of the sea, even as ships once

51

sailed between the boots of the famous Colossus at old Rhodes. There you stand, lost in the infinite series of the sea, with nothing ruffled but the waves. The tranced ship indolently rolls; the drowsy trade winds blow; everything resolves you into languor."

But there is a danger in all this seductive oneness. Simply feeling good about life doesn't mean life is good. "But while this sleep, this dream is on ye," Ishmael continues, "move your foot or hand an inch; slip your hold at all; and your identity comes back in horror. Over Descartian vortices you hover. And perhaps, at mid-day, in the fairest weather, with one half-throttled shriek you drop through that transparent air into the summer sea, no more to rise for ever. Heed it well, ye Pantheists!"

With the appearance of Ahab on the quarterdeck, everything changes. Ishmael becomes one not with the cosmos but with his captain's monomaniacal quest. Ishmael may have his intellectual pretensions, but they evaporate in the face of Ahab's overwhelming charisma. "[M]y oath had been welded with [the rest of the crew's]," Ishmael admits. "A wild, mystical, sympathetical feeling was in me; Ahab's quenchless feud seemed mine."

Ishmael insists, however, that he did not totally succumb to an Ahab view of the world. Ahab's hunt for Moby Dick is based on hatred. "He piled upon the whale's white hump the sum of all the general rage and hate felt by his whole race from Adam down; and then, as if his chest had been a mortar, he burst his hot heart's shell upon it." Ishmael, on the other hand, is more afraid than angry, and true to his aesthetically sensitive, essentially Romantic nature; he is most frightened not by the size and strength of Moby Dick but by his distinctive color. "It was the whiteness of the whale that above all things appalled me," he says.

What ensues in chapter 42, "The Whiteness of the Whale," is the antithesis of the Nantucket chapter. Instead of rhetorical elation, the point is complete and total depletion. Whiteness evokes, Ishmael insists, "the demonism in the world." It "shadows forth the heartless voids and immensities of the universe, and thus stabs us from behind with the thought of annihilation." It is "a dumb blankness, full of meaning, . . . a colorless, all-color of atheism." Even worse, the whiteness of the whale suggests that the whole visible world, the world of beauty and of love, is a fraud: "[T]he sweet tinges of sunset skies and woods; yea, and the gilded velvets of butterflies, and the butterfly cheeks of young girls; all these are but subtle deceits, not actually inherent in substances, but only laid on from without; so that all deified Nature absolutely paints like the harlot, whose allurements cover nothing but the charnel-house within. . . . [P]ondering all this, the palsied universe lies before us a leper. . . . And of all these things the Albino whale was the symbol. Wonder ye then at the fiery hunt?"

It is with this chapter that Ishmael loses his faith, his nerve, his confidence. He comes down from the inspiring heights of the topmast and, like everyone aboard the *Pequod,* is drawn irresistibly into Ahab's angry, iron-grooved way.

Ishmael's transformation echoes what was happening to the northern portion of the United States when Melville was working on *Moby-Dick*. During the fall of 1850 and the winter of 1851, Boston became the epicenter of outrage over the Fugitive Slave Law, and Melville's father-in-law, Judge Lemuel Shaw, was the reluctant focal point. Although Shaw hated slavery, he also loved his country and its laws, which it was his duty to uphold. So it was Shaw who ordered that a slave who'd made his way to Boston be turned over to his Southern captors. Riots and general bedlam erupted, with Shaw being hanged in effigy after the decision. New England gentlemen who had once viewed the South from the safety of their own mastheads had finally been drawn into slavery's pernicious vortex. What to do?

Nothing, of course. As Starbuck discovers, simply being a good guy with a positive worldview is not enough to stop a force of nature like Ahab, who feeds on the fears and hatreds in us all. "My soul is more than matched," Starbuck laments, "she's overmanned; and by a madman!" Just like Starbuck, America's leaders in the 1850s looked at one another with vacant, deer-in-the-headlights stares as the United States, a great and noble country crippled by a lie, slowly but inevitably sailed toward its cataclysmic encounter with the source of its discontents.

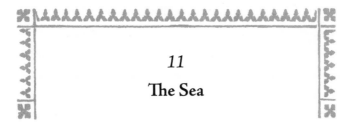

11
The Sea

We Americans love our wilderness: that empty space full of beckoning dreams, the unknown land into which we can disappear, only to return years later, wiser, care-worn, and rich. Most of us think of the West as this hinterland of opportunity, but Melville knew that the original wilderness was the "everlasting terra incognita" of the sea. Even today, long after every terrestrial inch of the planet has been surveyed and mapped, only a small portion of the sea's total volume has been explored by man. Back in 1850, Melville commented that "Columbus sailed over numberless unknown worlds to discover his one superficial western one."

Today the American West is a place of cities, suburbs, ghost towns, and national parks. It is civilized. Not so the sea. "[H]owever baby man may brag of his science and skill," Ishmael ominously intones, "and however much, in a flattering future, that science and skill may augment; yet for ever and for ever, to the crack of doom, the sea will insult and murder him, and pulverize the stateliest, stiffest frigate he can make; nevertheless, by the continual repetition of these very impressions, man has lost that sense of the full awfulness of the sea which aboriginally belongs to it." This is not the sea of the "Nantucket" chapter. This is the godless sea of the *Essex* disaster. "No mercy, no power but its own controls it . . . ," Ishmael continues; "the masterless ocean overruns the globe . . . the universal cannibalism of the sea; all whose creatures prey upon each other, carrying on eternal war since the world began."

Given the dangers of the ocean, the wisest thing for a man or woman to do is to steer for the same Polynesian islands that the *Essex* men so feared and to remain there at all costs. "For as this appalling ocean surrounds the verdant land, so in the soul of man there lies one insular Tahiti, full of peace and joy, but encompassed by all the horrors of the half known life. God keep thee! Push not off from that isle, thou canst never return!"

Ishmael's "insular Tahiti" is the South Seas equivalent of a 1960s-style fallout shelter; both are hideouts from "the horrors of the half known life," radioactive or wet. The United States in the 1850s must have felt much as it did during the cold war. In both eras, citizens lived with the conviction that a catastrophe was imminent. America dodged the nuclear bullet in the 1960s, but the twenty-first century feels more and more like an era in which a cataclysm, whether financial, environmental, or terrorist devised, is just around the corner. In the end, we are still at the mercy of the sea.

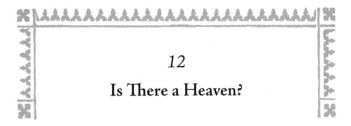

12

Is There a Heaven?

To love and work and be happy in this life is to refrain from focusing on what awaits us and everyone we care about: decay and death, at least in this world. The curse of being human is to realize that it all ends and can do so at any moment. To acknowledge and internalize this truth in an unmediated way is to go, like Ahab, insane.

Some people don't think about death very much, if at all. Since there's nothing they can do about it, why worry about it? Not Melville. Judging from his letters to Hawthorne and his writings throughout his life, he thought about it all the time. The belief that death was the end, that we are utterly and truly annihilated when we die, was not something he could easily accept. He desperately needed to know there is a heaven.

In the beginning of the book, Ishmael is confident that eternity will be waiting for him no matter what happens down here on Earth. He may be crushed by a whale, but not even God can stave his immortal soul. Even before the *Pequod* sets sail, however, he has begun to wonder whether this is entirely true. It becomes an obsessive theme of *Moby-Dick:* Is there a heaven?

At one point Ishmael jokingly tells us how he proposes to settle the question once and for all with the help of a whale: "With a frigate's anchors for my bridle-bitts and fasces [bundles] of harpoons for spurs, would I could mount that whale and leap the topmost skies, to see whether the fabled heavens with all their countless tents really lie encamped beyond my mortal sight!"

Later in the book, in his description of the ship's carpenter, who is called upon to manufacture Ahab's new whalebone leg, Melville provides a haunting portrayal of a world bereft of heaven. The carpenter is an existential nullity without a spark of intelligence or human warmth; he merely exists. He personifies a world without God. His "impersonal stolidity . . . seemed one with the general stolidity discernible in the whole visible world," Ishmael tells us, "involving, too, as it appeared, an all-ramifying heartlessness . . . ; living without premeditated reference to this world or the next . . . ; his brain, if he had ever had one, must have early oozed along into the muscles of his fingers."

Ahab is infuriated by his dependence on the carpenter. "Here I am," he agonizingly soliloquizes, "proud as a Greek god, and yet standing debtor to this blockhead for a bone to stand on!" He may strive to transcend all that is mundane and bestial, but in the end Ahab is a one-legged old man who requires the help of others.

So it was for Melville, an author with unquenchable ambition, but who depended on mere mortals to publish and read his books. "What I feel most moved to write, that is banned,—it will not pay," he lamented to Hawthorne. "Yet, altogether, write the *other* way I cannot. So the product is a final hash, and all my books are botches. . . . What's the use of elaborating what, in its very essence, is so short-lived as a modern book?" But, of course, more than 150 years after its publication, we are still reading *Moby-Dick*. Posthumously, Melville achieved the promised land; he is a god in our literary pantheon.

In the summer of 1851, as he struggled to finish his whaling novel, Melville dared to imagine himself and Hawthorne together in a writers' paradise. They would find "some little shady corner by ourselves," and with a basket of champagne they would "cross our celestial legs in the celestial grass that is forever tropical, and strike our glasses and our heads together, till both musically ring in concert." They would then reminisce about their past lives and compose "humorous, comic songs" with titles such as "'Oh, when I lived in that queer little hole called the world,' or, 'Oh, when I toiled and sweated below,' or, 'Oh, when I knocked and was knocked in the fight.'" As the agnostic writing outside his own uncertain beliefs, Melville is describing the fantasy he desperately needed but could never quite convince himself existed. It is a paradise born of several longings: of the twelve-year-old boy for his dead father; of the author for fame; and of the almost-middle-aged man for a friend. It is the longing that is in all of us, and it is there, in every page of *Moby-Dick*.

13
A Mighty, Messy Book

Hawthorne had a lot to do with the making of *Moby-Dick*, but the novel truly began in February 1849 when Melville purchased a large-type edition of Shakespeare's plays. The eyes that would become so inflamed during the composition of *Moby-Dick* were already beginning to bother him. "[C]hancing to fall in with this glorious edition," he wrote to a friend of the large-type volumes, "I now exult over it, page after page."

Melville's example demonstrates the wisdom of waiting to read the classics. Coming to a great book on your own after having accumulated essential life experience can make all the difference. For Melville, the timing could not have been better, and in the flyleaf of the last volume of his seven-volume set of Shakespeare's plays are notes written during the composition of *Moby-Dick* about Ahab, Pip, and other characters.

Instead of being intimidated by Shakespeare, Melville dared to wonder whether he might be able to surpass him. Given the constraints that existed in Elizabethan England, Shakespeare had to be careful about what he revealed. As a result, Melville wrote, "[i]n Shakespeare's tomb lies infinitely more than Shakespeare ever wrote." Fully realizing his own age applied its own set of limitations on a writer, he still wondered whether being an American in the mid-nineteenth century might allow him to push the artistic bar set by Shakespeare to new heights. "[E]ven Shakespeare was not a frank man to the uttermost," he wrote to Duyckinck. "And, indeed, who in this intolerant Universe is, or can be? But the Declaration of Independence makes a difference."

Shakespeare was a critical influence on *Moby-Dick,* but there is also the Bible, which Melville, in essence, reimagined through the prism of his youthful experiences in the Pacific, providing his prose with an energy and surprise born of a convergence of the Old Testament and pagan exoticism even as he grappled with the issues of his own day. There is the Jonah of Father Mapple's sermon at the Seamen's Bethel in New Bedford, who, like a runaway slave in post–Fugitive Slave Act America, attempts to escape God's omniscient gaze but is stymied at every turn. "In this world . . . ," Father Mapple sermonizes, "sin that pays its way can travel freely, and without a passport; whereas Virtue, if a pauper, is stopped at all frontiers."

Embedded in the narrative of *Moby-Dick* is a metaphysical blueprint of the United States. Melville fills the book with telling similes and metaphors that allow a story set almost entirely at sea to evoke the look and feel of America in 1850. When rowing after a whale, Ahab's crew of five powerful oarsmen produce such force that they "started the boat along the water like a horizontal burst boiler out of a Mississippi steamer." After a whale has been cut up, the *Pequod*'s crew use block and tackle to "drag out [the] teeth, as Michigan oxen drag stumps of old oaks out of wild wood-lands." When a sperm whale's severed head accidentally drops back down into the sea, it hits "with a thunder-boom . . . like Niagara's Table-Rock into the whirlpool." The "thick curled bush of white mist" rising from a massive herd of sperm whales looks "like the thousand cheerful chimneys of some dense metropolis, descried of a balmy autumnal morning, by some horseman on a height." We are on the deck of the *Pequod* with Captain Ahab, but we are also visiting the scenes, commonplace and noteworthy, of inland America.

Despite *Moby-Dick*'s often dark and ominous themes, Melville obviously had great fun writing this book. Listen to him here as, tongue in cheek, he proclaims the novel's audacious scope. "Give me a condor's quill! Give me Vesuvius' crater for an inkstand! Friends, hold my arms! For in the mere act of penning my thoughts of this Leviathan, they weary me, and make me faint with their outreaching comprehensiveness of sweep, as if to include the whole circle of the sciences, and all the generations of whales, and men, and mastodons, past, present, and to come, with all the revolving panoramas of empire on earth, and throughout the whole universe, not excluding its suburbs. Such, and so magnifying, is the virtue of a large and liberal theme! We expand to its bulk. To produce a mighty book, you must choose a mighty theme. No great and enduring volume can ever be written on the flea, though many there be who have tried it." *Moby-Dick* is a true epic, embodying almost every powerful American archetype as it interweaves creation myths, revenge narratives, folktales, and the conflicting impulses to create and to destroy, all played out across the globe's vast oceanic stage.

There is a wonderful slapdash quality to the book. Melville inserts chapters of biology, history, art criticism, you name it, sometimes at seeming random. Ishmael is the narrator, but at times Melville invests him with an authorial omniscience. It's a violation of the supposed laws of fiction writing; but who cares? In this book, especially the chapter titled "Cetology," which contains some of the funniest parody writing you'll ever find, Melville is out to lay bare his own creative process as well as the absurdity of our attempts to classify and quantify our lives into manageable, understandable entities. "[T]hough of real knowledge there be little," Ishmael confides, "yet of books there are a plenty." Ishmael creates a ridiculously complex classification system for whales but is finally left trying to account for some species that don't fit in his system, dismissing these unclassifiable whales as "full of Leviathanism, but signifying nothing." Like Melville's book, Ishmael's "cetological System" can never be fully completed. "For small erections may be finished by their first architects," he declares; "grand ones, true ones, ever leave the copestone to posterity. God keep me from ever completing anything.

A Mighty, Messy Book

This whole book is but a draught—nay, but the draught of a draught. Oh, Time, Strength, Cash, and Patience!"

Even the beginning of the book is a magnificent mess. Contrary to what many people assume, *Moby-Dick* starts not with Ishmael but with "Etymology," a listing of obscure quotations and translations supposedly collected by "a late consumptive usher to a grammar school." As if that's not enough, Melville follows "Etymology" with "Extracts," a seemingly endless compilation of whale-related passages that takes up a full thirteen pages in the Penguin edition of the novel. From the beginning, Melville is challenging the reader with both his scholarship and his wit. By the time you reach chapter 1, you know you are in for a most quirky and demanding ride.

There is an inevitable tendency to grow impatient with the novel, to want to rush and even skip over what may seem like yet another extraneous section and find out what, if anything, is going to happen next to Ahab and the *Pequod*. Indeed, as the plot is left to languish and entire groups of characters vanish without a trace, you might begin to think that the book is nothing more than a sloppy, self-indulgent jumble. But Melville is conveying the quirky artlessness of life through his ramshackle art. "[C]areful disorderliness," Ishmael assures us, "is the true method."

For me, *Moby-Dick* is like the Oldsmobile my grandparents owned in the 1970s, a big boat of a sedan with loosey-goosey power steering that required constant back-and-forth with the wheel to keep the car pointed down the highway.

Melville's novel is that wandering, oversized automobile, each non sequitur of a chapter requiring its own course correction as the narrative follows the erratic whims of Melville's imagination toward the Pacific. The sheer momentum of the novel is a wonder to behold, barreling us along, in spite of all the divergences, toward the White Whale.

14

Unflinching Reality

Within weeks of meeting Melville in August 1850, Hawthorne had procured copies of the young novelist's two latest books, *Redburn* and *White-Jacket*. Both were based on Melville's own experiences at sea: *Redburn* recounts his first voyage as a common seaman from New York City to Liverpool and back; *White-Jacket* tells of his stint aboard the naval frigate that took him from Hawaii to Boston. Hawthorne read the novels, his wife, Sophia, recounted to Evert Duyckinck, "on the new hay in the barn—which is a delightful place for the perusal of worthy books." In a letter of his own to Duyckinck, Hawthorne spoke of his "progressive appreciation" of Melville's work. "No writer ever put the reality before his reader more unflinchingly," he wrote.

Melville's great strength (a strength that sometimes got lost in his Ahab-like preoccupation with what he once called "ontological heroics") was an almost journalistic ability to record the reality of being alive at a particular moment. In *Moby-Dick* we feel in a profoundly emotional and visceral way what it was like to be a whaleman in the nineteenth century. In the chapter titled "The Affidavit," Melville makes it clear that what he is describing could really have happened. The reality of whaling is, he insists, more incredible than anything a novelist could invent. "So ignorant are most landsmen of some of the plainest and most palpable wonders of the world," he writes, "that without some hints touching the plain facts, historical and otherwise, of the fishery, they might scout at Moby Dick as a monstrous fable, or still worse and more detestable, a hideous and intolerable allegory."

Ishmael points to several historical instances, including the story of the *Essex,* that illustrate "the great power and malice at times of the sperm whale." Clearly, a whale is no ship's carpenter. Far from passive and dull, a bull whale not only is huge but also thinks with the crafty intelligence of a man.

Ishmael describes the wondrous way a craft as tiny as a whaleboat negotiates the massive swells of the ocean: "[T]he sudden profound dip into the watery glens and hollows; the keen spurrings and goadings to gain the top of the opposite hill; the headlong, sled-like slide down its other side;—all these, with the cries of the headsmen and harpooneers, and the shuddering gasps of the oarsmen . . . all this was thrilling." And then there is the even more wondrous way a whale dives underneath the sea: "[T]he monster perpendicularly flitted his tail forty feet into the air, and then sank out of sight like a tower swallowed up."

No one has ever written a more beautiful and horrifying account of the death of a whale than the magnificent set piece contained in chapter 61, "Stubb Kills a Whale." Perched on the onrushing bow of the whaleboat, the second mate merrily probes for "the life" of the whale with his lance until the giant creature begins to die. "His tormented body rolled not in brine but in blood, which bubbled and seethed for furlongs behind in their wake. The slanting sun playing upon this crimson pond in the sea, sent back its reflection into every face, so that they all glowed to each other like red men." The whale goes into its final paroxysms, "spasmodically dilating and contracting his spout-hole, with sharp, cracking, agonized respirations. At last, gush after gush of clotted red gore, as if it had been the purple lees of red wine, shot into the frighted air; and falling back again, ran dripping down his motionless flanks into the sea. . . . Stubb scattered the dead ashes [of his pipe] over the water; and, for a moment, stood thoughtfully eyeing the vast corpse he had made."

In his detailed descriptions of the whale's anatomy, Melville is carefully, meticulously preparing us for the novel's climax. In the chapter titled "The Battering-Ram," Ishmael anatomizes the "compacted collectedness" of the sperm whale's block-shaped head. It is, he tells us, "a dead, blind wall, . . . [an] enormous boneless mass . . . as though the forehead of the Sperm Whale were paved with horses' hoofs. I do not think that any sensation lurks in it." In addition to this mysterious "wad" of insensitivity, we are introduced to the whale's tiny and "lashless eye, which you would fancy to be a young colt's eye; so out of all proportion is it to the magnitude of the head." The spout hole is "countersunk into the summit of the whale's head" so that "even when tranquilly swimming through the mid-day sea in a calm, with his elevated hump sun-dried as a dromedary's in the desert; even then, the whale always carries a small basin of water on his head, as under a blazing sun you will sometimes see a cavity in a rock filled up with rain." The whale's tail is "a dense webbed bed of welded sinews . . . knit over with a warp and woof of muscular fibres and filaments . . . so that in the tail the confluent measureless force of the whole whale seems concentrated to a point. Could annihilation occur to matter, this were the thing to do it . . . where infantileness of ease undulates through a Titanism of power."

Reading *Moby-Dick,* we are in the presence of a writer who spent several impressionable years on a whaleship, internalized everything he saw, and seven or so years later, after internalizing Shakespeare, Hawthorne, the Bible, and much more, found the voice and the method that enabled him to broadcast his youthful experiences into the future. And this, ultimately, is where the great, unmatched potency of *Moby-Dick,* the novel, resides. It comes from an author who not only was there but possessed the capacious and impressionable soul required to appreciate the wonder of what he was seeing. At one point, Ishmael draws our attention to the majestic head of the sperm whale: "[G]azing on it . . . ," he insists, "you feel the Deity and the dread powers more forcibly than in beholding any other object in living nature. . . . If hereafter any highly cultured, poetical nation shall lure back to their birth-right, the merry May-day gods of old; and livingly enthrone them again in the now egotistical sky; in the now unhaunted hill; then be sure, exalted to Jove's high seat, the great Sperm Whale shall lord it."

By the last third of the novel, we know all there is to know about the anatomy of the whale and the specifics of killing a whale; we have also come to appreciate the whale's awe-inspiring mystery and beauty. As a consequence, Melville is free to describe the final clash between Ahab and Moby Dick with the unapologetic specificity required to make an otherwise improbable and overwrought confrontation seem astonishingly real.

15
Poetry

Moby-Dick is a novel, but it is also a book of poetry. The beauty of Melville's sentences is such that it sometimes takes me five minutes or more to make my way through a single page as I reread the words aloud, feeling the rhythms, the shrewdly hidden rhymes, and the miraculous way he manages consonants and vowels. Take, for example, this passage from chapter 51, "The Spirit-Spout," which picks up with the *Pequod* just south of St. Helena: "while gliding through these latter waters that one serene and moonlight night, when all the waves rolled by like scrolls of silver; and, by their soft, suffusing seethings, made what seemed a silvery silence, not a solitude: on such a silent night a silvery jet was seen far in advance of the white bubbles at the bow. Lit up by the moon, it looked celestial; seemed some plumed and glittering god uprising from the sea."

Good poetry is not all about lush and gorgeous words. It's about creating an emblematic and surprising scene that opens up new worlds. When the *Pequod* meets the whaleship *Albatross,* the men at the mastheads find themselves passing each other silently in the sky: "Standing in iron hoops nailed to the mast, they swayed and swung over a fathomless sea; and though, when the ship slowly glided close under our stern, we six men in the air came so nigh to each other that we might almost have leaped from the mast-heads of one ship to those of the other; yet, those forlorn-looking fishermen, mildly eyeing us as they passed, said not one word to our own look-outs, while the quarter-deck hail was being heard from below."

Good poetry also directs our attention to the most ordinary of human experiences. I know that I cannot go to bed on a cold winter night without thinking of Ishmael's lyrical aside in chapter 11, "Nightgown," about the benefits of sleeping in an unheated room. Not only does he provide some very practical advice; he delivers a kind of poetics of physical sensation that culminates in a quietly stunning prose haiku. "[T]o enjoy bodily warmth," Ishmael explains, "some small part of you must be cold, for there is no quality in this world that is not what it is merely by contrast. Nothing exists in itself. If you flatter yourself that you are all over comfortable, and have been so a long time, then you cannot be said to be comfortable any more. But if . . . the tip of your nose or the crown of your head be slightly chilled, why then, indeed, in the general consciousness you feel most delightfully and unmistakably warm. For this reason a sleeping apartment should never be furnished with a fire, which is one of the luxurious discomforts of the rich. For the height of this sort of deliciousness is to have nothing but the blanket between you and your snugness and the cold of the outer air. Then there you lie like the one warm spark in the heart of an arctic crystal."

In chapter 60, "The Line," Ishmael's poetry takes something as prosaic as a piece of rope and turns it into a continuously evolving metaphor of the human condition. He begins with the differences between the two kinds of lines ("Hemp is a dusky, dark fellow, a sort of Indian; but Manilla is as a golden-haired Circassian to behold"), then describes how the line crisscrosses the whaleboat in "complicated coils, twisting and writhing around it . . . in its perilous contortions," which leads to a description of what happens when the whale is harpooned and the line darts out ("like being seated in the midst of the manifold whizzings of a steam-engine in full play, when every flying beam, and shaft, and wheel, is grazing you") and then to the final revelation: "All men live enveloped in whale-lines. All are born with halters round their necks; but it is only when caught in the swift, sudden turn of death, that mortals realize the silent, subtle, ever-present perils of life."

In chapter 85, "The Fountain," Ishmael's description of a whale's spout causes him to launch into a riff about the figurative steam that sometimes emanates from his own skull, what he calls "a curious involved worming and undulation in the atmosphere over my head . . . while plunged in deep thought, after six cups of hot tea in my thin shingled attic." In this instance, the image leads to a philosophical breakthrough in which Ishmael hits upon the attitude with which all of us should confront this conundrum called life: "[R]ainbows do not visit the clear air; they only irradiate vapor. And so, through all the thick mists of the dim doubts in my mind, divine intuitions now and then shoot, enkindling my fog with a heavenly ray. . . . Doubts of all things earthly, and intuitions of some things heavenly; this combination makes neither believer nor infidel, but makes a man who regards them both with equal eye." A generous agnostic, Ishmael is also a witty and profound poet for whom enlightenment comes from the improvisational magic of words.

16
Sharks

Darkness has fallen by the time the second mate Stubb's freshly killed whale is secured to the side of the *Pequod*. Even though it is already quite late, Stubb decides he wants a whale steak for supper. He rouses the ship's black cook, Fleece, from his hammock and orders him to prepare the bloody hunk of whale meat. As Stubb mercilessly harasses the old man about how to cook the steak, hordes of hungry sharks enjoy a meal of their own in the dark waters below: "[T]housands on thousands of sharks, swarming round the dead leviathan, smackingly feasted on its fatness. The few sleepers below in their bunks were often startled by the sharp slapping of their tails against the hull, within a few inches of the sleepers' hearts. Peering over the side you could just see them . . . wallowing in the sullen, black waters, and turning over on their backs as they scooped out huge globular pieces of the whale of the bigness of a human head. . . . The mark they thus leave on the whale, may best be likened to the hollow made by a carpenter in countersinking for a screw."

It is a terrifying and fascinating scene in which Melville

lays bare the brutal savagery that underlies even the most polite of slave-master relationships. Stubb claims the uproar in the waters below is bothering him and orders Fleece to address the sharks. While delivered in a stilted dialect, the sermon that follows contains wisdom that comes straight from the author himself. "Your woraciousness, fellow-critters, I don't blame ye so much for; dat is natur, and can't be helped; but to gobern dat wicked natur, dat is de pint. You is sharks, sartin; but if you gobern de shark in you, why den you be angel; for all angel is not'ing more dan de shark well goberned."

This is Melville's ultimate view of humanity, the view he will bring to brilliant fruition forty years later in the novella *Billy Budd*. The job of government, of civilization, is to keep the shark at bay. All of us are, to a certain degree, capable of wrongdoing. Without some form of government, evil will prevail.

Here lies the source of the Founding Fathers' ultimately unforgivable omission. They refused to contain the great, ravening shark of slavery, and more than two generations later their grandchildren and great-grandchildren were about to suffer the consequences.

17

The Enchanted Calm

Even amid the worst of all possible worlds, life goes on. Even amid the dehumanizing brutality of Southern slavery and the agony of a concentration camp, people find a refuge, if only temporarily, from the suffering and fear. In chapter 87, "The Grand Armada," Melville takes us to that secret center within the storm. It's that place where passion and love can bloom, even in the most horrible of circumstances; otherwise the human race (which has known plenty of rough patches) would have long since ceased to exist.

Shortly after escaping Malaysian pirates, the *Pequod* comes upon a massive pod of whales. When the whales realize they are under attack, some of them flee in a "distraction of panic." Others simply give up in a "strange perplexity of inert irresolution" and are easily killed. This mixture of panic and paralysis was typical of a group of whales that had become, in the words of the whalemen, "*gallied*." Rather than be surprised by the behavior, Ishmael reminds us that "there is no folly of the beasts of the earth which is not infinitely outdone by the madness of men." All of us, whales and men alike, have our absurdities, especially when our fears get the better of us.

Ishmael's whaleboat crew harpoons a whale that drags them ever deeper into the chaotic fury of the gallied herd. Eventually, "the direful disorders seemed waning," and they enter "the innermost heart of the shoal . . . [where] the sea presented that smooth satin-like surface, called a sleek. . . . Yes, we were now in that enchanted calm which they say lurks at the heart of every commotion."

Within this lake-like still point, all the rules have changed. Instead of hunter and prey, it is as if the whalemen and the whales are now part of the same extended family. "[I]t almost seemed that some spell had suddenly domesticated them," Ishmael recounts. "Queequeg patted their foreheads; Starbuck scratched their backs with his lance." At the center of this benign and blissful scene, a mother whale suckles her baby. Melville, the new father, engrafts the physical delicacy of his infant son into his account of a newborn whale: "The delicate side-fins, and the palms of his flukes, still freshly retained the plaited crumpled appearance of a baby's ears newly arrived from foreign parts." Elsewhere whales are gently copulating. "Some of the subtlest secrets of the seas seemed divulged to us in this enchanted pond," Ishmael tactfully relates.

Melville has created a portrait of the redemptive power of intimate human relations, what he calls elsewhere "the wife, the heart, the bed, the table, the saddle, the fire-side, the country." It is an ideal that would sadly elude him for much of his married life. His professional frustrations seem to have made him a difficult husband; at one point things got so bad that Lizzie's family considered intervening on her behalf. His relationship with his children, especially his sons, was also filled with tension. Like "young Stiggs" of the Try Pots Inn on Nantucket, his oldest child, Malcolm, a baby during the composition of *Moby-Dick*, would be found dead in his room from a self-inflicted gunshot wound at the age of eighteen. Nineteen years later, Melville's younger son, Stanwix, died alone in a hospital room in San Francisco at the age of thirty-five.

During the winter and spring of 1851, however, Melville still dared to believe in the possibility of familial happiness. No matter how troubling the news about the riots in Boston might be, no matter how disappointing his book sales, he could count on the unalloyed pleasures of hearth and home. "And thus," Ishmael says of this inner circle of cetacean contentment, "though surrounded by circle upon circle of consternations and affrights, did these inscrutable creatures at the centre freely and fearlessly indulge in all peaceful concernments; yea, serenely revelled in dalliance and delight. But even so, amid the tornadoed Atlantic of my being, do I myself still for ever centrally disport in mute calm; and while ponderous planets of unwaning woe revolve round me, deep down and deep inland there I still bathe me in eternal mildness of joy."

And then it all goes to hell. A whale tangled in the line of a deadly cutting spade works his way through the pod, "wounding and murdering his own comrades" with every agonized

sweep of his tail. What Ishmael next describes eerily anticipates the gradual collapse of Melville's own family life—not to
mention America's fated slide into war. "First, the whales
forming the margin of our lake began to crowd a little, and
tumble against each other, as if lifted by half spent billows
from afar; then the lake itself began faintly to heave and swell;
the submarine bridal-chambers and nurseries vanished; in
more and more contracting orbits the whales in the more cen-
tral circles began to swim in thickening clusters. Yes, the long
calm was departing. A low advancing hum was soon heard;
and then like to the tumultuous masses of block-ice when the
great river Hudson breaks up in Spring, the entire host of
whales came tumbling upon their inner centre, as if to pile
themselves up in one common mountain. Instantly Starbuck
and Queequeg changed places; Starbuck taking the stern."
The hunt is on.

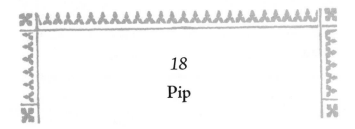

18
Pip

With his tambourine and kindly, laughing eyes, Pip, the black cabin boy, is a favorite of the crew. Unfortunately, he is also afraid of whales. When Stubb's after-oarsman sprains his hand, Pip is ordered to join the second mate's whaleboat crew. It does not go well. When a harpooned whale thwacks the boat, Pip leaps up in fright and becomes entangled in the whale line, forcing Tashtego to release the whale.

Stubb is not happy. "Stick to the boat, Pip," he commands, "or by the Lord, I wont pick you up. . . . We can't afford to lose whales by the likes of you; a whale would sell for thirty times what you would, Pip, in Alabama." In eerily modern words, Ishmael comments, "[T]hough man loves his fellow, yet man is a money-making animal, which propensity too often interferes with his benevolence." Suffice it to say that Pip soon jumps again and falls into the sea.

"It was a beautiful, bounteous, blue day," Ishmael recounts, "the spangled sea calm and cool, and flatly stretching away, all round, to the horizon, like gold-beater's skin hammered out to the extremest. Bobbing up and down in that sea,

Pip's ebon head showed like a head of cloves. No boat-knife was lifted when he fell so rapidly astern. Stubb's inexorable back was turned upon him; and the whale was winged. In three minutes, a whole mile of shoreless ocean was between Pip and Stubb. Out from the centre of the sea, poor Pip turned his crisp, curling, black head to the sun, another lonely cast-away, though the loftiest and the brightest."

Anyone who has swum out from a boat floating on the ocean or even on a large lake has felt the panic of realizing that below you is an emptiness so vast that you in your pitiful churnings are nothing. You are completely and absolutely alone. "The intense concentration of self in the middle of such a heartless immensity," Ishmael says, "my God! who can tell it?" Pip lives the *Essex* nightmare in all its heartbreaking, wisdom-gathering poignancy, providing the *Pequod* with, Ishmael informs us, "a living and ever accompanying prophecy of whatever shattered sequel might prove her own."

Pip's mind and soul, if not his body, travel down into the distant depths of a sea that Ishmael elsewhere describes as "the tide-beating heart of earth." Down there at the bottom, "strange shapes of the unwarped primal world glided to and fro before his passive eyes; and the miser-merman, Wisdom, revealed his hoarded heaps; and among the joyous, heartless, ever-juvenile eternities, Pip saw the multitudinous, God-omnipresent, coral insects, that out of the firmament of waters heaved the colossal orbs. He saw God's foot upon the treadle of the loom, and spoke it; and therefore his shipmates called him mad. So man's insanity is heaven's sense; and wandering from all mortal reason, man comes at last to that celestial thought, which, to reason, is absurd and frantic; and weal or woe, feels then uncompromised, indifferent as his God." Pip is eventually saved, but he is left a husk, an idiot savant of eternity, to whom Ahab in his angry attempt to get at the source of our collective human misery is inevitably drawn.

As the innocent victim who sees too much, Pip becomes the counter to Ahab's other confidant, Fedallah. Whereas the Parsee, an amalgam of Iago and the Weird Sisters of *Macbeth*, whispers teasing prophecies in Ahab's ear, Pip is part cipher, part sounding board. Like King Lear's Fool, Pip proves that Ahab has, in the words of one of the *Pequod*'s owners, "his humanities."

19
The Squeeze

There are two ways to get oil out of a sperm whale. You can peel off the blubber, chop it into bits, and boil it into oil. Then there is the creature's blocklike head, which Ishmael jokingly refers to as the great Heidelburgh Tun: a huge reservoir of vodka-clear oil known as spermaceti. Once the spermaceti is exposed to the air, it begins to solidify, "sending forth beautifully crystalline shoots," Ishmael informs us, "as when the first thin delicate ice is just forming in water." Eventually, the spermaceti (so named because that's what it now looks like, semen or sperm) becomes so thick and lumpy that it must be squeezed back into a liquid form before it can be heated in the tryworks.

For Ishmael, the antidote to Pip's terrible loneliness is sitting around a big tub of spermaceti with his shipmates as they all squeeze the gooey, sticky, mushy clumps and, inevitably, each other's hands. You can just see the crinkle in those small penetrating eyes as Melville pushed this not-so-subtle double entendre into the kinds of places Walt Whitman would go just four years later with the publication of *Leaves of Grass* in 1855.

"Oh! my dear fellow beings," Ishmael effuses, "why should we longer cherish any social acerbities, or know the slightest ill-humor or envy! Come; let us squeeze hands all round; nay, let us all squeeze ourselves into each other; let us squeeze ourselves universally into the very milk and sperm of kindness." This is the homoerotic answer (which, given his troubled marriage, may have been where Melville's heart really lay) to the heterosexual bliss of "The Grand Armada."

As it turns out, chapter 94, "A Squeeze of the Hand," is just a warm-up for the next chapter, "The Cassock," in which Melville constructs what may be the most elaborate, not to mention obscene, pun in all of literature. Ishmael begins by describing how the mincer, the sailor who cuts up the whale blubber into thin pieces known as bible leaves, secures a very special coat made from—get this—the foreskin of a sperm whale's penis . . . that's right, the foreskin of a whale. I won't go into the details (for that you have to read the book), but suffice it to say that once the mincer is dressed in this black tubular outfit, he looks, Ishmael insists, just like a clergyman as he stands at a pulpit-like table slicing the blubber into bible leaves. It's then that Ishmael delivers the punch line. "[W]hat a candidate for an archbishoprick," he enthuses, "what a lad for a Pope were this mincer!"

20

The Left Wing

When I was growing up in Pittsburgh in the 1960s, we would sometimes drive into the city past the steel mills along the Monongahela River. The stench and smoke were so bad that my younger brother and I would hold our breath as we looked in fascination at those scorched towers belching fire. Twenty or so years later, when I moved to Nantucket and became interested in the island's whaling past, I came to realize that Nantucket in the early nineteenth century, when the town was the center of America's first global industry, was much more like the Pittsburgh of my childhood than the posh summer resort it had become. Back in the nineteenth century, Nantucket stank of oil, and in 1846, when a fire broke out at a hat store on Main Street, close to half the town was consumed by flames fed by the very element that had sustained the island for more than a hundred years. Nantucket rebuilt, this time in brick, but for all intents and purposes whaling was finished. Within a couple of decades the island's population had dropped from ten thousand to just three thousand. Nantucket was on its way to becoming a ghost town, just as my old home Pittsburgh has been abandoned by a sizable segment of its population since it, too, lost the industry that once made it famous. It's what happens to communities, large or small, afloat or ashore, that play with fire.

To kindle a fire on an oil-soaked wooden ship was risky at best, but it was the only way to boil the blubber into oil. Wood was used to start the fire in the brick tryworks, but once the rendering of the blubber had begun, the flames were fed with the crispy bits that floated to the top of the bubbling try-pots. This meant that the fire that consumed the whale was fed with pieces of the whale's own body. The smoke that poured forth from this organically fueled flame smelled even worse than the fumes from burned human hair. According to Ishmael, "It has an unspeakable, wild, Hindoo odor about it, such as may lurk in the vicinity of funereal pyres. It smells like the left wing of the day of judgment; it is an argument for the pit."

This horrible smoke wafts across the deck as Ishmael stands at the *Pequod*'s helm on a dark and breezy night. "[T]he wild ocean darkness was intense," he recounts. "But that darkness was licked up by the fierce flames, which at intervals forked forth from the sooty flues, and illuminated every lofty rope in the rigging, as with the famed Greek fire. The burning ship drove on, as if remorselessly commissioned to some vengeful deed. . . . [T]he rushing Pequod, freighted with savages, and laden with fire, and burning a corpse, and plunging into that blackness of darkness, seemed the material counterpart of her monomaniac commander's soul." Ishmael is taken over by a "stark, bewildered feeling, as of death" as he attempts to steer the *Pequod* through her self-created fog. Suddenly he discovers that he has somehow managed to turn himself around so that he is now facing the stern instead of the bow. This means that any turn of the helm will be the opposite of what he intends and could very well capsize the ship. Ishmael quickly corrects himself. "How glad and how grateful the relief from this unnatural hallucination of the night," he says.

There is a lesson in all of this. "Give not thyself up, then, to fire, lest it invert thee, deaden thee; as for the time it did me," Ishmael advises. "There is a wisdom that is woe; but there is a woe that is madness." What is needed more than anything else in the midst of a crisis is a calm, steadying dose of clarity, the kind of omniscient, all-seeing perspective symbolized by an eagle on the wing: "And there is a Catskill eagle in some souls that can alike dive down into the blackest gorges, and soar out of them again and become invisible in the sunny spaces. And even if he for ever flies within the gorge, that gorge is in the mountains; so that even in his lowest swoop the mountain eagle is still higher than other birds upon the plain, even though they soar." Here Melville provides a description of the ideal leader, the anti-Ahab who instead of anger and pain relies on equanimity and judgment, who does his best to remain above the fray, and who even in the darkest of possible moments resists the "woe that is madness."

As I have said before, *Moby-Dick* is a book that was written for the future. In this portrait of a person who resists the fiery, disorienting passions of the moment, who has the soul of a high-flying Catskill eagle, Melville, in his preternatural way, has hit upon a description of the political figure America desperately needed in 1851 but who would not appear on the national stage until almost a decade later, when Abraham Lincoln became president of the United States.

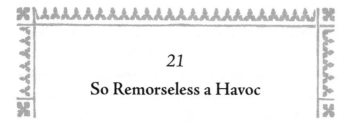

21

So Remorseless a Havoc

In chapter 105, Melville tackles a prescient question given today's extinction-prone Earth: "whether Leviathan can long endure so wide a chase, and so remorseless a havoc; whether he must . . . , like the last man, smoke his last pipe, and then himself evaporate in the final puff." In the paragraphs that follow, Ishmael compares the whale to the buffalo in the American West and acknowledges that given what has happened to those "humped herds," it might seem inevitable that "the hunted whale cannot now escape speedy extinction."

But after examining the question from a variety of angles, he decides that this is not the case. First off, whales have a much larger habitat than the buffalo—larger, in fact, than all the earth's landmasses combined. Second, sperm whales have the ability to retreat to "their Polar citadels" in the icy north and south, where they can "bid defiance to all pursuit from man." As a consequence, the whale is, Ishmael insists, "immortal in his species, however perishable in his individuality."

For those of us who grew up in the aftermath of the industrialized slaughter of whales in the 1950s and 1960s, when it looked as if several species of cetaceans would indeed go the way of the buffalo, Ishmael might seem woefully naive, especially since the world's ice sheet has so dramatically diminished in recent years. On the other hand, the sperm whale population is now on the rebound even as evidence continues to mount that our addiction to what replaced whale oil—petroleum—has contributed to global warming and sea-level rise. In the years to come, the combination of climate change and population growth could have a devastating effect on the planet and, needless to say, on humanity. Maybe Ishmael's reference to "the last man" is more than a figure of speech. Instead of whales, maybe the endangered megafauna is us.

"In Noah's flood [the whale] despised Noah's Ark," Ishmael reminds us, "and if ever the world is to be again flooded, like the Netherlands, to kill off its rats, then the eternal whale will still survive, and rearing upon the topmost crest of the equatorial flood, spout his frothed defiance to the skies." There it is, Ishmael's vision of the future: a drowned world devoid of land dwellers, a paradise for whales.

22

Queequeg

In *Typee,* the bestseller Melville wrote about his time with the native peoples of the Marquesas, the narrator is at first enraptured with his hosts, in particular the beautiful Fayaway. But then something strange happens. His leg begins to bother him to the point that he can no longer walk. He soon realizes that he must leave this island paradise; otherwise he is going to rot to death like an old banana. "Try to go back to the savages," the novelist D. H. Lawrence wrote in an essay about Melville, "and you feel as if your very soul was decomposing inside you." So what happens when the roles are reversed; what happens when the native flees his island paradise for a whaleship?

Queequeg was born on a Pacific island but decided that he had to leave. Like Melville, he fled his former home for the strangeness of the other. After his years as a whaleman, he is no longer strictly a native, but he is far from being your ordinary Westerner. He is, Ishmael tells us, "a creature in the transition state—neither caterpillar nor butterfly." And then, after several sweltering days cleaning out the *Pequod*'s hold, this tattooed exotic from the South Seas gets sick and, like the narrator in *Typee,* begins to die.

As his body wastes away, his eyes become increasingly prominent. "[L]ike circles on the water, which, as they grow fainter, expand; so his eyes seemed rounding and rounding, like the rings of Eternity. An awe that cannot be named would steal over you as you sat by the side of this waning savage, and saw as strange things in his face, as any beheld who were bystanders when Zoroaster died."

When Queequeg was on Nantucket, he saw, Ishmael relates, "certain little canoes of dark wood . . . ; and upon inquiry, he . . . learned that all whalemen who died in Nantucket, were laid in those same dark canoes." Since his own people laid out their dead in canoes, he decided that he, too, should be buried in a "coffin-canoe," and the carpenter subsequently builds him one of these formfitting vessels with some old planks taken from a grove of trees on a South Seas island named, cunningly enough, Lackaday.

Like the *Essex* crew members, who fitted out their own coffin-canoes with what provisions they salvaged from the wreck, Queequeg prepares his craft for a voyage to eternity, requesting that his harpoon, some biscuits, a flask of water, a bag containing "woody earth scraped up in the hold," and a piece of folded sailcloth for a pillow be placed in the coffin. Once all is in readiness and Queequeg has climbed into the coffin to make sure it is "a good fit," he suddenly begins to feel better. "[I]t was Queequeg's conceit," Ishmael says, "that if a man made up his mind to live, mere sickness could not kill him." Within a few days, Queequeg is fully recovered and decides to use his coffin-canoe as a sea chest. Later in the novel, after the *Pequod*'s life buoy is lost during an unsuccessful attempt to save a sailor who has fallen from the rigging, Queequeg offers his sea chest as a replacement. And so his former coffin-canoe is caulked and sealed and turned into a life buoy, the irony of which is not lost on Ahab. "A life-buoy of a coffin!" he soliloquizes. "Does it go further? Can it be that in some spiritual sense the coffin is, after all, but an immortality-preserver! I'll think of that."

Queequeg, the instigator of this unsettling transformation, remains an enigma to the end. The tattoos on his body were etched by one of his island's holy men "who, by those hieroglyphic marks, had written out . . . a complete theory of the heavens and the earth, and a mystical treatise on the art of attaining truth; so that Queequeg in his own proper person was a riddle to unfold; a wondrous work in one volume; but whose mysteries not even himself could read."

For Ahab, who spends his days and nights ruminating on the meaning of the universe, Queequeg's mere presence is a torment, providing hints but no answers in his eternal quest for certainty. One morning, Ishmael recounts, Ahab turns from the harpooneer with a frustrated cry: "Oh, devilish tantalization of the gods!"

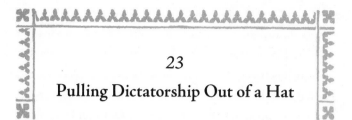

23

Pulling Dictatorship Out of a Hat

Just about anyone, it turns out, can be a demagogue or a dictator if he or she masters a few simple tricks, what Ishmael calls "some sort of external arts and entrenchments, always, in themselves, more or less paltry and base." As a result, most leaders "become famous more through their infinite inferiority to the choice hidden handful of the Divine Inert, than through their undoubted superiority over the dead level of the mass." Dictators such as Adolf Hitler and Saddam Hussein are not geniuses; they are power-hungry, paranoid, and expert manipulators of men. If you want to understand how these and other megalomaniacs pull it off, read the last third of *Moby-Dick* and watch as Ahab tightens his stranglehold on the *Pequod*'s crew through a series of magic tricks worthy of Las Vegas.

It begins with the sacrilegious forging of the harpoon meant to kill Moby Dick ("'Ego non baptizo te in nomine patris, sed in nomine diaboli!' deliriously howled Ahab, as the malignant iron scorchingly devoured the baptismal blood"). Then Ahab tramples his quadrant ("Science! Curse thee, thou vain toy") and waves around his demonically glowing harpoon during a terrifying storm only to blow out the lurid fire with his own hot breath. Finally, there is the equally dramatic magnetizing of a new compass needle to replace the one blasted by lightning. The cumulative effect of these over-the-top acts of prestidigitation is a purposeful numbing of the crew's (and, it must be admitted, the reader's) emotions as all of us become servile automatons to Ahab's unalterable purpose: "Alike, joy and sorrow, hope and fear, seemed ground to finest dust, and powdered, for the time, in the clamped mortar of Ahab's iron soul. Like machines, they dumbly moved about the deck, ever conscious that the old man's despot eye was on them."

There are occasional brief reprieves when the *Pequod* meets yet another whaleship with news of Moby Dick (each ship representing its own alternative to the Ahab way), but as the final showdown approaches, we have become so scorched and crushed and otherwise slapped around by Ahab in his magnificent emergence as an evil superhero that it becomes increasingly difficult to care.

But that is precisely the point.

24

Essex Redux

We all struggle with the demands of work. We need the money to support ourselves and our families, but when does a job, especially the pat on the back for a job well done, begin to distract us from the much more difficult work of being a good parent and spouse? If you want to understand how a job can destroy a person, read not only *Moby-Dick* but the real-life story that underlies much of the latter portion of the novel.

In April 1851, just about the time Melville was entering the final stages of writing *Moby-Dick,* he received a copy of Owen Chase's narrative of the *Essex* disaster, the same book he had read a decade before as a whaleman in the Pacific. The Chase narrative had come via a Nantucket friend of his father-in-law's, and this may have been the first time he'd read the account (which had become quite rare) since his introduction to the story in the forecastle of the *Acushnet.* Just as he was writing notes to himself in the back pages of his volumes of Shakespeare's plays, Melville wrote down relevant memories of his connection to the *Essex* in the Chase volume.

In addition to recounting how he came to read the book for the first time, he writes about seeing none other than Owen Chase himself during a gam with the ship *Charles Carroll.* (Historians have since established that Melville was mistaken in this claim, but for our purposes the important point is that Melville *thought* he saw Chase.) "He was a large, powerful well-made man; rather tall . . . with a handsome face for a Yankee, & expressive of great uprightness & calm unostentatious courage. His whole appearance impressed me pleasurably. He was the most prepossessing-looking whale-hunter I think I ever saw." But like the captain of the *Essex,* George Pollard, whose bad luck continued when his next command struck an uncharted reef off Hawaii and sank, "the miserable pertinaciousness of misfortune . . . did likewise hunt poor Owen, tho' somewhat more dilatory in overtaking him, the second time." Melville heard that soon after the gam with the *Acushnet,* Chase received "letters from home, informing him of the certain infidelity of his wife, the mother of several children. . . . We also heard that this receipt of this news had told most heavily upon Chase, & that he was a prey to the deepest gloom."

What moves Melville now, ten years after first reading Chase's narrative, is the personal plight of the participants. Not mere symbols, Chase and Pollard are men who have been bludgeoned by fate. There is a pathos, even a tenderness, that enters *Moby-Dick* in its final chapters, and it was Melville's memory of the real men behind the *Essex,* Nantucketers who never completely escaped the shadow of that disaster, that brought a much-needed injection of humanity to his attempts to bring his dangerously digressive, sometimes bombastic novel to a close.

It begins with chapter 128, when the *Pequod* meets the *Rachel,* whose captain has halted his pursuit of whales to search for the missing whaleboat containing his son. In this heartbreaking chapter, in which the captain unsuccessfully pleads with Ahab to assist him in his search, we see the terrifying coldness behind Ahab's quest for Moby Dick. It is not until chapter 132, "The Symphony," however, that all the sadness and despair of Melville's notes in the Chase narrative, particularly when it comes to the fragility of domestic happiness, come to the fore in Ahab's conversation with the conscience of the *Pequod,* Starbuck.

The chapter begins on the quarterdeck on the morning of a beautiful "steel-blue day." Ahab is alone, looking out across the serene Pacific. "That glad, happy air, that winsome sky, did at last stroke and caress him; the step-mother world, so long cruel—forbidding—now threw affectionate arms round his stubborn neck, and did seem to joyously sob over him, as if over one, that however wilful and erring, she could yet find it in her heart to save and to bless." It is then that a tear leaks from Ahab's eye and falls into the sea. At that moment Starbuck comes upon the captain and pauses on the quarterdeck. Suddenly noticing the first mate, Ahab launches into a lament about the purposelessness of his purpose-driven life.

We learn that he is fifty-eight years old and of the forty years he's been a whaleman, he has spent not even three ashore. "When I think of this life I have led," he tells Starbuck, "the desolation of solitude it has been; the masoned, walled-town of a Captain's exclusiveness . . . oh, weariness! heaviness! Guinea-coast slavery of solitary command!—when I think of all this . . . how for forty years I have fed upon dry salted fare—fit emblem of the dry nourishment of my soul!" He is married and has a son, but what good is that given his commitment to the hunt? "I widowed that poor girl when I married her." Like all of us wedded to our careers, whether we be doctors, teachers, truckers, lawyers, bond traders, or writers, he has missed what is truly important: "[W]hat a forty years' fool—fool—old fool, has old Ahab been! Why this strife of the chase? why weary, and palsy the arm at the oar, and the iron, and the lance? how the richer or better is Ahab now?"

Starbuck sees his chance. "Oh, my Captain! my Captain! noble soul! grand old heart, after all! why should any one give chase to that hated fish! Away with me! let us fly these deadly waters! let us home! Wife and child, too, are Starbuck's. . . . How cheerily, how hilariously, O my Captain, would we bowl on our way to see old Nantucket again! I think, sir, they have some such mild blue days, even as this, in Nantucket."

But Ahab, all his strength and will drained out of him, is ultimately powerless to alter the momentum established after forty long years as a whaleman. "What is it, what nameless, inscrutable, unearthly thing is it; what cozening, hidden lord and master, and cruel, remorseless emperor commands me; that against all natural lovings and longings, I so keep pushing, and crowding, and jamming myself on all the time; recklessly making me ready to do what in my own proper, natural heart, I durst not so much as dare?"

Starbuck eventually gives up and walks away. When Ahab crosses the quarterdeck and looks once again into the sea, he discovers with a start that another pair of eyes are reflected in the ocean's windless surface—those of the evil puppet master, Fedallah. Starbuck, we realize, never had a chance.

This is where Melville is perhaps the most profound in his portrait of Ahab as the demagogue and dictator. In the end, even the fiercest of tyrants is done in, not by his own sad, used-up self, but by his enablers, the so-called professionals, who keep whispering in his ear.

25

The Inmost Leaf

In his letters to Hawthorne, Melville provides snapshots of his psyche during and after the composition of his masterpiece. The same propulsive poetry that animates *Moby-Dick* runs through these missives, many of them wildly manic in their intimate revelations of what Melville was thinking about as his novel galloped, paused, then galloped again toward publication. I would go so far as to insist that reading *Moby-Dick* is not enough. You must read the letters to appreciate the personal and artistic forces that made the book possible.

By early May, Melville was almost through with the novel he was then calling *The Whale*. Then he stopped writing. In early June he tells Hawthorne that for the last three weeks he had been "out of doors,—building and patching and tinkering away in all directions. Besides, I had my crops to get in,—corn and potatoes . . . and many other things to attend to, all accumulating upon this one particular season. I work myself; and at night my bodily sensations are akin to those I have so often felt before, when a hired man, doing my day's work from sun to sun."

The hiatus has apparently been good for his creative energies, if not his sanity. Melville begins to sound like someone gone giddy on truth serum as he discloses his most intimate concerns. He frets about his literary reputation: "To go down to posterity is bad enough, any way; but to go down as a 'man who lived among the cannibals'!" He worries that his book is a meandering "botch" even as he fears that it signals the end of a five-year period of exhilarating intellectual growth: "Until I was twenty-five, I had no development at all. From my twenty-fifth year I date my life. Three weeks have scarcely passed, at any time between then and now, that I have not unfolded within myself. But I feel that I am now come to the inmost leaf of the bulb, and that shortly the flower must fall to the mould." In a week, he tells Hawthorne, he will go to New York City "to bury myself in a third-story room, and work and slave on my 'Whale' while it is driving through the press. *That* is the only way I can finish it now,—I am so pulled hither and thither by circumstances. The calm, the coolness, the silent grass-growing mood in which a man *ought* always to compose,— that, I fear, can seldom be mine." A few paragraphs later, he returns to the subject of his novel: "But I was talking about the 'Whale.' As the fishermen say, 'he's in his flurry' when I left him some three weeks ago. I'm going to take him by his jaw, however, before long, and finish him up in some fashion or other."

Here we see Melville marshaling the courage for one last go-around with the White Whale. Like Ahab, he is about to go into battle, and like Ahab, who spills his soul to Starbuck in "The Symphony," Melville tells Hawthorne everything. He fears, more than anything else, that this is the end of something; already he can sense that his artistic powers will never again reach this height, and it terrifies him. For three weeks, he has been plowing his land, pounding nails with a hammer, his mind turning over the final encounter with Moby Dick, and the result will be one of the most exciting and intricately choreographed action sequences ever written.

26

Ahab's Last Stand

Before we continue, I need to make something perfectly clear. The White Whale is not a symbol. He is as real as you or I. He has a crooked jaw, a humped back, and a wiggle-waggle when he's really moving fast. He is a thing of blubber, blood, muscle, and bone—a creation of the natural world that transcends any fiction. So forget about trying to figure out what the White Whale signifies. As Melville has already shown in chapter 99, "The Doubloon," in which just about every member of the *Pequod*'s crew provides his own interpretation of what is stamped on the gold coin nailed to the mast, in the end a doubloon is just a doubloon. So don't fall into the Ahab trap of seeing Moby Dick as a stand-in for some paltry human complaint. In the end he is just a huge, battle-scarred albino sperm whale, and that is more than enough.

This is the fundamental reason we continue to read this or any other literary classic. It's not the dazzling technique of the author; it's his or her ability to deliver reality on the page.

Which leads us to yet another blessing provided by Melville's reengagement with the *Essex* narrative in the spring of

1851. In Chase's unforgettable firsthand account, he told of what it was like to be aboard a ship that had become the target of a giant whale's wrath. With Chase's words fresh in his memory, Melville launched into a series of scenes that conveyed an unmatched sense of immediacy even as they nimbly gathered together the many strands of the novel's narrative.

In chapter 133, "The Chase—First Day," Melville divides our introduction to Moby Dick into three parts. We first see him from a distance, moving leisurely across the surface of the sea as the *Pequod*'s whaleboats, led by Ahab, approach. "As they neared him, the ocean grew still more smooth; seemed drawing a carpet over its waves; seemed a noon-meadow, so serenely it spread. At length the breathless hunter came so nigh his seemingly unsuspecting prey, that his entire dazzling hump was distinctly visible, sliding along the sea as if an isolated thing, and continually set in a revolving ring of finest, fleecy, greenish foam. . . . A gentle joyousness—a mighty mildness of repose in swiftness, invested the gliding whale. . . . [N]ot Jove, not that great majesty Supreme! did surpass the glorified White Whale as he so divinely swam." This is Moby Dick as aesthetic object: a slithering snowhill projecting circles of glorious calm.

Then the whale starts to dive, and we realize that there is more to this big white creature than at first met the eye. "But soon the fore part of him slowly rose from the water; for an instant his whole marbleized body formed a high arch, like Virginia's Natural Bridge, and warningly waving his bannered flukes in the air, the grand god revealed himself, sounded, and went out of sight." And we wait. For an hour. The tension builds, and then in a scene that inverts even as it anticipates the black vortex that will soon consume the *Pequod*, Ahab stares into the endless watery blue and sees Moby Dick. Note the cinematic nature of how we are there with Ahab as he looks down into the aquamarine void: "[S]uddenly as he peered down and down into its depths, he profoundly saw a white living spot no bigger than a white weasel, with wonderful celerity uprising, and magnifying as it rose, till it turned, and then there were plainly revealed two long crooked rows of white, glistening teeth, floating up from the undiscoverable bottom."

Ahab somehow escapes the White Whale's first attempt to capture the boat in his jaws, but not the second. Moby Dick rolls onto his back like an attacking shark and seizes the boat in his mouth "so that the long, narrow, scrolled lower jaw curled high up into the open air. . . . The bluish pearl-white of the inside of the jaw was within six inches of Ahab's head. . . . In this attitude the White Whale now shook the slight cedar as a mildly cruel cat her mouse. With unastonished eyes Fedallah gazed, and crossed his arms; but the tiger-yellow crew were tumbling over each other's heads to gain the uttermost stern."

Fedallah may be sitting there like a diabolical Yoda, but not Ahab. "[T]hen it was that monomaniac Ahab, furious with this tantalizing vicinity of his foe, which placed him all alive and helpless in the very jaws he hated; frenzied with all this, he seized the long bone with his naked hands, and wildly strove to wrench it from its gripe." In our age, we all love whales and wish them nothing but the best, but you've got to hand it to this castrated, one-legged, fifty-eight-year-old lapsed Quaker; he doesn't mess around. Like Melville with *his* Whale, he has the audacity to take Moby Dick by the jaw. "As now he thus vainly strove, the jaw slipped from him; the frail gunwales bent in, collapsed, and snapped, as both jaws, like an enormous shears, sliding further aft, bit the craft completely in twain, and locked themselves fast again in the sea, midway between the two floating wrecks."

Now that Ahab is in the water, Moby Dick sticks his head up into the air and starts revolving like a lighthouse beacon so that he can see what's around him. (As Melville points out in a footnote, this is a common behavior among sperm whales. No matter how fantastic it may seem, everything in these last three chapters *could* have happened.) What Moby Dick sees, it turns out, is Ahab, who quickly finds himself at the center of a wild maelstrom of whale-induced foam. Luckily, the *Pequod* isn't too far away. "Sail on the whale!—Drive him off!" Ahab shouts.

The ship succeeds in pushing back Moby Dick, and Ahab is hauled into Stubb's whaleboat, where he lies "all crushed in the bottom . . . like one trodden under foot of herds of elephants." Instead of a man, Ahab is a piece of topography, a fractured continent echoing hurt and pain. "Far inland, nameless wails came from him," Ishmael tells us, "as desolate sounds from out ravines."

On Day Two of the encounter, Moby Dick bashes Stubb's and Flask's whaleboats to bits before diving below the surface. In the swirling wake of the White Whale's leave-taking, the second and third mates and their crews cling desperately to whatever is close at hand as "the odorous cedar chips of the wrecks danced round and round, like the grated nutmeg in a swiftly stirred bowl of punch." Thanks to Melville's letter to Hawthorne, we know how personal this scene is to him. "My dear Sir, a presentiment is on me," Melville wrote. "I shall at last be worn out and perish, like an old nutmeg-grater, grated to pieces by the constant attrition of the . . . nutmeg." In the destruction of two whaleboats, Melville is also portraying the disintegration of his talent.

Day Three dawns clear and fresh, and the narrative takes a breather. "What a lovely day again!" Ahab marvels. "[W]ere it a new-made world, and made for a summer-house to the angels, and this morning the first of its throwing open to them, a fairer day could not dawn upon that world." He then lapses into a soliloquy that echoes Melville's complaint to Hawthorne that he has rarely known the quiet circumstances required to produce proper creative writing. "Thinking is, or ought to be," Ahab says, "a coolness and a calmness; and our poor hearts throb, and our poor brains beat too much for that." Here Melville touches on that dynamic tension between active and passive engagement. If the author simply sits back like God and casts judgment, the verdict is inevitably less than persuasive. What makes for good writing is when the author somehow achieves perspective within the tumult of the moment, and this is exactly what Melville accomplishes in *Moby-Dick*.

But back to Ahab, who happens to have good reason to be agitated. Amid the chaotic furor of the previous day's action, Fedallah mysteriously disappeared. What makes this particularly ominous is that the harpooneer had prophesied that he must die and then reappear before Ahab could be killed. Instead of dwelling on this *Macbeth*-like riddle, Ahab soon finds himself rowing through a sea of ravenous sharks that, like the nutmeg grater, chew the blades of his oars into fragments.

It all comes together like Fate's well-oiled machine: Fedallah's lifeless body appears among the snarl of harpoon lines crisscrossing the White Whale's humped back; as Fedallah also predicted, Moby Dick then transforms the *Pequod* into a vast, American-built hearse when the whale bashes into her bow with his mammoth head. As the ship sinks into the sea, Ahab hurls his harpoon only to have the line wrap around his neck and whisk him to his death in the wake of the creature he despised above all else. Lastly, there is the Wampanoag harpooneer Tashtego at the masthead, valiantly fulfilling Ahab's order to nail his bloodred flag to the top of the spar even as a savage sky hawk attempts to steal away the flag. The sky hawk's wing becomes caught between the masthead and Tashtego's hammer (one wonders whether Melville came up with this astonishing conclusion as he hammered away at his house that spring) and is pulled down with the *Pequod,* "which, like Satan, would not sink to hell till she had dragged a living part of heaven along with her, and helmeted herself with it."

The chapter concludes by reaching back to Noah even as it anticipates America's blood-soaked day of reckoning to come: "Now small fowls flew screaming over the yet yawning gulf; a sullen white surf beat against its steep sides; then all collapsed, and the great shroud of the sea rolled on as it rolled five thousand years ago."

After the titanic fury of the final three chapters, the epilogue comes as an immense relief. Ishmael, it turns out, was the one who replaced Fedallah in Ahab's whaleboat. Luckily, he and several others were tossed from the boat prior to the captain's death and watched the final scene from the edges of the fray. Once the ship sank and the ensuing vortex began to drag all of them under, Queequeg's coffin life buoy popped up out of the water, and Ishmael became the *Pequod*'s only survivor. "Buoyed up by that coffin, for almost one whole day and night, I floated on a soft and dirge-like main. The unharming sharks, they glided by as if with padlocks on their mouths; the savage sea-hawks sailed with sheathed beaks. On the second day, a sail drew near, nearer, and picked me up at last." Magically preserved in the predator-free zone of "The Grand Armada," Ishmael is rescued by the *Rachel,* still in search of her captain's missing son. This means that instead of elation, Ishmael brings only disappointment to his rescuers. "It was the devious-cruising Rachel, that in her retracing search after her missing children, only found another orphan." And so Melville ends his masterpiece with a tender presentiment of his own abandonment by both his audience and the man to whom he would dedicate the novel, Nathaniel Hawthorne.

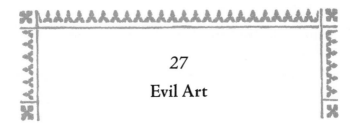

27

Evil Art

Melville had a hard time shaking the Ahab out of him. It would take a critical pummeling, the loss of his shy muse, and other disappointments before he came back down to earth again and realized that even after the miracle of *Moby-Dick*, nothing had really changed. But in early November 1851, within days of the novel's publication, he still believed in the power of his black art. Not only had his book come from the real world; it controlled that world.

On November 6, he received a letter from his New York friend Evert Duyckinck informing him of the sinking of the New Bedford whaleship *Ann Alexander* by a whale. "Your letter received last night had a sort of stunning effect on me," Melville wrote. "For some days past being engaged in the woods with axe, wedge, & beetle [a mallet], the Whale had almost completely slipped me for the time (& I was the merrier for it) when Crash! comes Moby Dick himself . . . & reminds me of what I have been about for part of the last year or two. . . . I make no doubt it *is* Moby Dick himself, for there is no account of his capture after the sad fate of the Pequod about fourteen years ago." Melville was only half kidding. After comparing the *Ann Alexander* whale to the literary critics who were about to bash his book ("What he has to say is short & pithy & very much to the point"), he let slip a startling admission: "I wonder if my evil art has raised this monster."

28

Neither Believer nor Infidel

Poor Nathaniel Hawthorne. Back in the summer of 1850 he had hoped to avoid being introduced to Melville. A little over a year later, Melville had dedicated a book to him. What was this timid, withdrawn writer to do? Get out of town, that's what. But before he and his family beat a hasty retreat from the Berkshires to the suburbs of Boston, he wrote Melville a letter praising *Moby-Dick*. Hawthorne's letter no longer exists, but judging from Melville's response, the words were heartfelt. And, in fact, in the months ahead Hawthorne would write to Duyckinck, "What a book Melville has written! It gives me an idea of much greater power than his preceding ones."

Whatever Hawthorne wrote, his "joy-giving and exultation-breeding letter" was exactly what Melville needed to hear. "A sense of unspeakable security is in me this moment," he wrote, "on account of your having understood the book." But even before he finished the letter, "this infinite fraternity of feeling" had begun to fade. "My dear Hawthorne, the atmospheric skepticisms steal into me now, and make me doubtful of my sanity in writing you thus. But, believe me, I am not mad. . . . [T]ruth is ever incoherent, and when the big hearts strike together, the concussion is a little stunning." Even if *Moby-Dick* was now done and Hawthorne was about to leave him, perhaps what the two of them had shared during the last year would somehow endure. "I shall leave the world, I feel, with more satisfaction for having come to know you. Knowing you persuades me more than the Bible of our immortality."

The critics (including his friend Duyckinck) were not kind to *Moby-Dick,* but Melville pushed on, writing *Pierre,* a very strange novel about a tortured writer and his family that conveys a stupefying sense of spiritual claustrophobia but not much else. Then that summer, in July 1852, Melville traveled with his father-in-law, Judge Shaw, to Nantucket Island.

Imagine it: a year after writing *Moby-Dick,* Melville visited the island that served as the launching pad for his great, unappreciated masterpiece. At some point, he met Captain George Pollard, master of the *Essex.* "To the islanders he was a nobody," Melville later wrote in the back pages of his Chase narrative; "to me, the most impressive man, tho' wholly unassuming, even humble—that I ever encountered." Now that the excitement of creating *Moby-Dick* had faded, Melville was most impressed not by an ungodly, godlike Ahab but by a quiet, reserved survivor who had learned to live with disappointment. For someone who has ceased to believe in his own immortality (and as we shall soon see, Melville had reached that point), life isn't about achieving your dreams; it's about finding a way to continue in spite of them.

And then, during this trip to the islands south of Cape Cod, Melville was told a story by a lawyer friend of his father-in-law's that hit him like a thunderbolt, a story about a woman named Agatha Hatch who married a sailor, had his child, and proceeded to live without the sailor for seventeen years. As the lawyer (who happened to be the attorney general of Massachusetts) wrote to Melville, the story of Agatha was "a most striking instance of long continued & uncomplaining submission to wrong and anguish on the part of a wife, which made her in my eyes a heroine."

Melville decided that this was just the "skeleton of actual reality" for a novel, especially if it were set on Nantucket, which instead of being a place of boisterous pluck had become by 1852 an island of whalers without whales. What's more, Agatha would have a George Pollard–like figure for a father: "a man of the sea, but early driven away from it by repeated disasters. Hence, is he subdued & quiet & wise in his life. And now he tends a light house, to warn people from those very perils, from which he himself has suffered." But then Melville did something pathetic. He wrote up a detailed précis and offered the story to Nathaniel Hawthorne, claiming that his friend would do a better job with it than he would.

When Hawthorne balked, Melville decided it was a good excuse to travel to Concord, Massachusetts, where Hawthorne and his family had since relocated. Not surprisingly,

Hawthorne urged Melville to write the story himself, which he subsequently decided to do. "I invoke your blessing upon my endeavors," he wrote hopefully; "and breathe a fair wind upon me." But the wind was anything but fair. The following spring, after completing a novel that seems to have been based on the story of Agatha titled *The Isle of the Cross,* Melville was "prevented" from publishing it, possibly because the publisher feared that the novel's similarity to actual events might invite a lawsuit. From then on, Melville (who appears to have destroyed the manuscript) would do his best to disguise what Hawthorne had recognized was his greatest strength: the unflinching portrayal of reality.

By that time Hawthorne's former roommate at Bowdoin College, Franklin Pierce, had become president of the United States. After writing Pierce's campaign biography (which one wag described as "the greatest work of fiction he ever wrote"), Hawthorne received a plum political appointment and was named U.S. consul in Liverpool, England. Melville, once again, would not be so lucky. Even though his family members and friends (including Hawthorne) campaigned heroically for him, he was offered nothing. By 1856, his family had become worried about his sanity and health, and Melville departed, alone, on a tour of Europe and the Holy Land. Soon after arriving in England, he traveled to Liverpool to visit Hawthorne.

It was November, and the two friends went for a walk on the beach in the windy sunshine. They found a sheltered spot amid the dunes and sat down for a smoke. "Melville, as he always does, began to reason of Providence and futurity," Hawthorne recorded in his journal, "and of everything that lies beyond human ken, and informed me that he had 'pretty much made up his mind to be annihilated'; but still he does not seem to rest in that anticipation; and, I think, will never rest until he gets hold of a definite belief. It is strange how he persists—and has persisted ever since I knew him, and probably long before—in wandering to and fro over these deserts, as dismal and monotonous as the sand hills amid which we were sitting. He can neither believe, nor be comfortable in his unbelief; and he is too honest and courageous not to try to do one or the other. If he were a religious man, he would be one of the most truly religious and reverential; he has a very high and noble nature, and better worth immortality than most of us."

Melville, Hawthorne recognized, was a man condemned to landlessness. There was no harbor for Melville, no refuge from the storm. For one brief year, with Hawthorne's friendship serving as his insular Tahiti, Melville dove down deeper than even Pip and came up with *Moby-Dick*. But instead of fame (at least in his own lifetime), *Moby-Dick* brought only obscurity. Instead of going down in a blaze of glory like Ahab, Melville went about his quiet, unassuming way like Captain Pollard.

No one knew it then, but Melville had created the literary equivalent of Queequeg's coffin life buoy: a book that vanishes into the depths only to explode to the surface just in the nick of time. What *Moby-Dick* needed, it turned out, was space—

the distance required for its themes and images to resonate unfettered by the turmoil and passions that had inspired them. Once free of its own historical moment, *Moby-Dick* became the seemingly timeless source of meaning that it is today.

But all that was in the distant future. In 1863, in the midst of the Civil War, Melville, his wife Lizzie, and their four children moved from the Berkshires back to New York City, where Melville worked as a customs inspector for close to two decades. After years of marital unhappiness, he and Lizzie appear to have reached an understanding, and in the 1880s they came into an inheritance. Without a need to work, Melville settled into his dark, book-lined room on Twenty-sixth Street in New York City and, with visits from his granddaughters serving as his chief distraction, continued his lifetime habit of reading and writing. When he died in 1891 at the age of seventy-two, he had completed his second masterpiece, *Billy Budd*.

After Melville's death, his family found a possible clue as to how he managed to survive the forty-year backwash left by the creation of *Moby-Dick* and, indeed, how he came to write that novel in the first place. Atop a table piled high with papers was a portable writing desk. Taped inside the desk, which had no bottom, was a piece of paper with a motto printed on it: "Keep true to the dreams of thy youth."

The phrase comes from the German poet and dramatist Friedrich Schiller, but what was its relevance to Melville? Late in life he wrote to his brother-in-law, "[A]t my years, and with my disposition, or rather, constitution, one gets to care less and less for everything except downright good feeling. Life is so short, and so ridiculous and irrational (from a certain point of view) that one knows not what to make of it, unless—well, finish the sentence for yourself." I propose that Melville would have finished that sentence with the words taped inside his writing desk.

In the end, Melville had found a way back to the view espoused by Ishmael in *Moby-Dick:* "Doubts of all things earthly, and intuitions of some things heavenly; this combination makes neither believer nor infidel, but makes a man who regards them both with equal eye." This redemptive mixture of skepticism and hope, this genial stoicism in the face of a short, ridiculous, and irrational life, is why I read *Moby-Dick*.

ACKNOWLEDGMENTS
AND READINGS

Many thanks to Kevin Doughten at Viking for being the first to ask the question that inspired me to write this book and that became its title. Thanks also to Wendy Wolf and Stuart Krichevsky for their input. I'd also like to thank the friends and family members who read and commented on the manuscript: Peter Gow, Susan Beegel, Mary K. Bercaw Edwards, Stuart Frank, Michael Hill, Richard Duncan, Thomas and Marianne Philbrick, and Melissa Philbrick. Thanks to Francesca Belanger for the wonderful design, to Jim Tierney for the cover, and to Bruce Giffords and Maggie Riggs for their help as well.

Below is a list of the works I consulted while writing this book. I am especially indebted to Andrew Delbanco's biography and its insights into the historical and political times in which Melville wrote. I was also deeply influenced by two Melville-related premieres: that of Jake Heggie and Gene Scheer's brilliant opera *Moby-Dick* in Dallas, Texas, in late

April 2010, and, a week and a half later, that of Ric Burns's equally distinguished film *Into the Deep* on PBS's *American Experience*.

Delbanco, Andrew. *Melville: His World and Work*. New York: Knopf, 2005.

Heflin, Wilson. *Herman Melville's Whaling Years*. Edited by Mary K. Bercaw Edwards and Thomas Farel Heffernan. Nashville: Vanderbilt University Press, 2004.

Hoare, Philip. *The Whale: In Search of the Giants of the Sea*. New York: Ecco, 2010.

Lawrence, D. H. *Studies in Classic American Literature*. 1923; New York: Viking, 1964.

Leyda, Jay. *The Melville Log: A Documentary Life of Herman Melville, 1819–1891*. 2 vols. New York: Harcourt, Brace, 1951.

Melville, Herman. *Correspondence*. Edited by Lynn Horth. Evanston and Chicago: Northwestern University Press and the Newberry Library, 1993.

———. "Hawthorne and His Mosses." In *The Piazza Tales and Other Prose Pieces, 1839–1860*. Edited by Harrison Hayford, Alma A. MacDougall, G. Thomas Tanselle, et al. Evanston and Chicago: Northwestern University Press and the Newberry Library, 1987.

———. *Moby-Dick; or, The Whale*. 1851; New York: Penguin Books, 2001.

Metcalf, Eleanor Melville. *Herman Melville: Cycle and Epicycle*. Cambridge, Mass.: Harvard University Press, 1953.

Olson, Charles. *Call Me Ishmael*. 1947; Baltimore: Johns Hopkins University Press, 1997.

Parker, Hershel. *Herman Melville: A Biography*. 2 vols. Baltimore: Johns Hopkins University Press, 1996 and 2002.

Philbrick, Nathaniel. "At Sea in the Tide Pool: The Whaling Town and America in Steinbeck's *The Winter of Our Discontent* and *Travels with Charley*." In *Steinbeck and the Environment*. Edited by Susan F. Beegel, Susan Shillinglaw, and Wesley N. Tiffney Jr. Tuscaloosa: University of Alabama Press, 1997.

———. "'Every Wave Is a Fortune': Nantucket Island and the Making of an American Icon." *New England Quarterly,* September 1993.

———. Foreword to *Moby-Dick; or, The Whale,* by Herman Melville. New York: Penguin Books, 2001.

———. "Hawthorne, Maria Mitchell, and Melville's 'After the Pleasure Party.'" *ESQ: A Journal of the American Renaissance* 37, no. 4 (1991).

———. *In the Heart of the Sea: The Tragedy of the Whaleship* Essex. New York: Viking, 2000.

———. "A Window on the Prey: The Hunter Sees a Human Face in Hemingway's 'After the Storm' and Melville's 'The Grand Armada.'" *Hemingway Review* (Fall 1994).

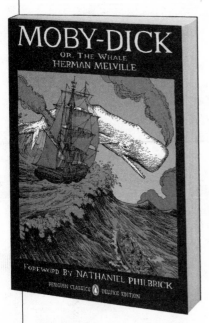